Gimmicks

Make Money In

Retailing

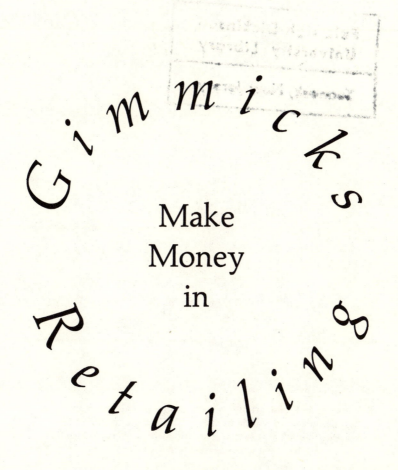

Gimmicks

Make
Money
in

Retailing

Second Edition

by *Betty Jane Minsky*

FAIRCHILD PUBLICATIONS
New York

TO

Gregg, Jenny, Ken, and Jack

Standard Book Number: 87005-095-8
Library of Congress Catalog Card Number: 71-153566

Printed in the United States of America

DESIGNED BY JEFFREY M. BARRIE

All photos are by the author except where otherwise credited.

Contents

Illustrations

Introduction

In the first edition of GIMMICKS MAKE MONEY IN RE-TAILING, I stated that in the past 50 years there had been a great change in retailing.

In the seven years since then, change has become a necessary aspect of retailing.

The retailer must not only adapt to change, but initiate change if he is to be a leader in the retailing scene of the 'seventies.

The mobile age brings customers from a greater area than ever before, but it also creates new problems. Competition is keen. Shopping centers vie with central business districts. Consumers are better educated, more aware. Legislation has become more restrictive. Tradition, life styles, and values are changing at a rapid rate.

Today's youth—the customers of both today and tomorrow—are making their wants and concerns known. They focus on the "total picture", with anxiety for the world of tomorrow their major concern, often replacing material wants.

Retailers can no longer remain an isolated entity content to mind their own affairs, the store, and just sell. Community obligations cannot be written off simply with an annual check to the Chamber of Commerce or participation in Christmas or white-sale events. Today's retailer must have a genuine concern for and interest in not only his customers but his community and its future as well. HE MUST MAKE THAT CONCERN AND INTEREST KNOWN.

Although there will always be new gimmicks, just plain "gim-micky" selling has about run its course. Today's customers, especially those in the younger age groupings (which comprise much of the market), demand more than "just another retail promotion". They'll shop a store because, they say, "We like it there," "He treats us nice," or "He cares." They reject another because, "He isn't fair," "doesn't like longhairs," "is prejudiced," "chased us out when we were in eighth grade," or simply because, "We don't like him."

Customers in the younger homemaking age bracket want stores that have facilities to entertain their children while they shop, even if these consist of just a simple play area; and stores that offer a place with tables and chairs to talk over anticipated purchases over coffee and cigarettes. No longer are these considered "extras"—they are services that today's shoppers take for granted, even demand.

Not only are today's customers interested in how they are treated, but they have an idealistic concern for others. Word spreads quickly through their grapevine.

In many instances, parents, especially younger ones, are expressing the same ideas. While they may have thought about these things before, now, led by their outspoken children, they are also voicing their concerns.

This is not to imply that there is no place for the novel gimmick in the retailing of the future.

BUT—THE GIMMICK WILL HAVE TO BE MORE NOVEL, MORE BRILLIANT, MORE ENTICING AND SHINE BRIGHTER IF IT IS TO PULL FOR ITS NOVELTY ALONE.

Enrich it with a host of other factors like store image, treatment of customers, community attitude, shopping convenience, customer services, fun and pleasant surroundings, and the novel gimmick can still be a tremendous drawing card.

Among the gimmicks gaining attention these days was one by a Dayton, Ohio, service station. To promote his car wash he advertised that airplanes would be washed free.

It happened!

One guy drove up with an airplane in tow.

The owner called for his crew.

The local news media was also alerted.

"It's on the house!" shouted the owner. He waved "happy landings" as the ingenious customer later drove away. The publicity and interest gained from that simple, inexpensive gimmick literally put the station on the map. No one can deny that the owner had imagination—and used it.

The first time it was a novelty.

Repeated it would be "Dullsville."

Customers can be gained from one-shot novelty efforts like that one. But they will later insist on fair pricing, good service, courteous treatment, and all of the other things they have a right to expect if they are to become repeaters.

The retailer who can employ that type of off-beat gimmick or launch a really spectacular promotion, and then couple it with good merchandising methods (many of which are gimmicks in themselves), is the retailer who indeed has found the GIMMICKS TO MAKE MONEY IN RETAILING.

Betty Jane Minsky

Foreword

How to Use Gimmicks in Retailing

As long as there remains a retailer with imagination and individuality, there will continue to be new gimmicks in merchandising.

Gimmicks are adaptable for any type of store, multi-store complex, or group of stores. Many can be used as novel methods of drawing attention to a particular promotion or event, or to the store itself. Others can help provide better service or a better image; or they can solve problems. There is no end to the benefits for which gimmicks may be used.

Some are simple and can be staged with little advance preparation. Some can be used on the spur of the moment to give a doldrum period a boost. Others may take considerable pre-planning and elaborate preparation.

Gimmick ideas in this book may be used alone or combined, but they will work best when "personalized" with individual adaptations to meet specific store needs.

Although a gimmick is designed to pull customers for specific events this does not mean the basic idea cannot be employed successfully at another time.

Gimmicks are versatile.

Those in this book are varied and are designed to provide a stimulus for special promotional efforts. Some are geared to help solve retail problems, such as shortages of parking spaces. Others are aimed at gaining entire new groups of customers by attracting new industry and pay checks or by luring in tourist dollars. Some will help improve the image of an individual store, while others are designed to upgrade the image of the retail community at large.

The ideas are not meant to be lifted from the text and used as they are, but to serve as the basis from which to build and innovate. Each will require personalization, as no two stores are alike. That in itself will make every gimmick unique, even if other retailers use the same basic idea.

CHAPTER
1

What Makes a Promotion

What makes a promotion?

The answer is simple, yet complex.

MANY THINGS.

Planning is a main ingredient.

Included should be a goal and detailed plans on how to reach it.

Nothing should be left to chance.

Publicity, advertising, goodwill, mailing lists, types of customers to be attracted, the actual physical conditions in which the event will be held are all details to be explored and mapped out before the promotion is launched.

When more than one store is involved, planning becomes more complex. The entire success of the event hinges, of course, not on how well one job is done, but on how well all participants do their tasks.

All crinkles in the wrapping of the publicity and advertising package should be smoothed out. Firm plans, not just vague ideas to be agreed on later, should precede all actual advertising, publicity, and promotional efforts.

There are specific times when promotions are called for. Among these are periods of gift buying, like graduation and Christmas, seasonal changes, and pay days at local plants.

But promotions can be overdone. Keep from falling into that trap by using a promotional calendar. Often, when one of these is lacking, a store will acquire a reputation for holding "just another

1

one of their old sales." But, given a specific theme and purpose in the planning procedure, and just the right timing, stores or groups of stores can employ gimmicks to move merchandise, draw customers, and make a sale more than just another old sale.

Gimmicks during promotions should be geared to co-ordinate with the event and add to it; otherwise they may detract from it.

Advertising and Invitations

Generally, promotional events will be publicized in one of two ways: to the public at large if the event is open to everyone; or by invitation if it is to be a private sort of thing. Once the choice between these two is made, the following gimmicks can be helpful in planning effective advertising and publicity programs.

ANNOUNCEMENTS AND INVITATIONS

Store name, address, date or dates of promotion, hours, theme, and, if the event is informal, feature items and gimmicks which will arouse interest should be included in announcements and invitations.

FORMAL INVITATIONS

If the event is to be stately and dignified, formal invitations or announcements should be used. Keep details to a minimum. Consider embosed or engraved invitations. Mail a week in advance.

The gimmick to the formal event is to make customers feel they are distinguished—that the event itself has an "elite" or "special" significance. But note that another gimmick is to keep the public at large from becoming annoyed that others are receiving special recognition and privilege. If this factor is taken care of, then formal events for special customers can be useful.

Don't overdo them. If they become commonplace they lose their effectiveness.

INFORMAL INVITATIONS

These require at most a week's notice. The main thing is to get the word out—to make the public aware that something is going on.

TEASER ANNOUNCEMENTS

Build intrigue by using "teaser" announcements early. Use interesting ads or mailers announcing that something worth watching for is coming up. Every few weeks add more details. Stir interest by building curiosity. Momentum gains as time goes on.

Through it all, tell the public to circle the date on their calendars.

Top off the campaign with a big "now it can be told" announcement giving all details.

Record and Analyze Promotions

No promotional effort is complete without analysis or record keeping. This is a vital follow-up and useful for later promotional planning. Whether it has been good or bad, analyze each promotion immediately after the event, while things are vivid in your memory.

Keep the records simple. If they are complex and time consuming, even the most dedicated retailer may soon dispense with this important gimmick.

Inexpensive methods to simplify record keeping yet make it complete include:

KEEP CLOSE RECORDS

How was the opening, the middle, the end? Jot a note suggesting what can be done in future events to pick up lagging spots. What roles did cash and credit play?

Was there a difference in response which could be traced to advertising; were there certain gimmicks which drew better than others? Was weather a factor and, if so, what can be done on the spur of the moment in future events to offset this? Did a pay period of a local industry have an effect?

Jot these and similar local conditions down for later reference.

NOTE NOVEL IDEAS

Jot down novel ideas *as they come to mind* during the event or at other times through the year so they can be implemented in future events. If this is "left 'til later," the ideas will be forgotten.

INDEX-CARD SYSTEM

A simple index-card file, in chronological order, may be used to record promotions, with one section for new ideas.

WALLPAPER-BOOK REFERENCE FILE

A huge wallpaper sample book lends itself well to record keeping. Each ad can be pasted in. On it pen how the event pulled, factors considered important, success or failure, what changes might be made.

Because these will be pasted in chronologically, a quick flip through the book will make seasonal records easy to find.

NOTEBOOK

An offshoot of the above is to keep another book-type listing of promotions and specific information about them. A simple notebook will do. If it is looseleaf, inserts can be made.

You can keep new ideas in a separate section.

FILES

Don't overlook setting up a promotional filing system, even if it's only a section of a file drawer. This will make it possible to file advertisements and brochures without pasting them permanently. They can be taken out and easily referred to when planning other events. If each item is dated, it can be slipped back into its proper place quickly.

Separate file folders can be used for ideas to try. Newspaper clippings, brochures, and similar printed material from other sources dealing with promotional ideas can be kept and quickly found under this method.

Be Prepared for a Flop

Not everything will succeed. Even the best planned and most elaborately staged promotions sometimes go astray. So good planning should include ideas on how to stage a comeback if the promotion lags.

A trait that is a must for successful promotions is being able to recognize a flop.

Along with this is the necessity to be able to pull out of the unfortunate situation and turn the flop into a success before the end. Good planning can be an aid in this area.

HAVE SUBSTITUTE PLANS

The gimmick is to prevent flops from becoming disasters by having substitute or alternate plans.

Prepare a list of novel ideas while in the planning stage. These should be of the type that can be quickly added to stir interest if needed.

Plans should include advertising possibilities for additions which may have to be made. The changes themselves won't accomplish much if the potential customers aren't aware of them.

Television and radio may be necessary to get last-minute messages out.

LEARN FROM MISTAKES

When analyzing promotions, pinpoint what went wrong and eliminate those errors in the future.

What pulls for one store may bring disaster to another. What attracts customers at one time may fail to entice them at another time.

Careful analyses can reveal why a promotion failed to jell, and these determinations can be assets in future planning.

Checklist

It is impossible to draw up a set of plans and state definitely that, if they are followed, promotions will succeed.

The very individuality of each store, with its particular kinds of customers and potential customers, and of each community, makes this impossible.

But there is enough sameness about all promotions that some elements can be considered to be of standard importance in most events.

These include:

DATES

Pick a date and decide how long the event will last. Set opening and closing dates. Check to see that these are mentioned in all advertising.

AMPLE PLANNING TIME

Allow time to prepare fully for the event.

RAIN DATES

If the event will be outdoors, select a rain date and advertise it so customers will know about it in advance. This will cut advertising costs in event the promotion is postponed.

SUBSTITUTE PLANS

Make alternate plans. Be prepared to extend or change the event if need be. Alternate advertising plans should be made so this can be readily accomplished.

PRE-SALE EVENTS

Consider a pre-sale event for special customers. This is effectively publicized by private invitations. Advise the "preferred" customers they will have first chance at items which will later be made available to the public. The success of this is due to the feeling of status it gives. Keep it that way by using private invitations and no public advertising.

Frequently stores offer an added discount during the pre-sale activity.

NAME

Pick a catchy name or theme which can be used in ads, decor, prizes, invitations, even in special merchandise offerings. Often the name or theme can be the co-ordinating factor to tie all elements together.

MERCHANDISE

Unless a specific product is being pushed, or the event is a clearance type, have a variety of merchandise involved. Buy items exclusively because they tie in with the event. These will be one-time-only items, things not generally stocked.

If the event runs for several days, feature specific items on specific days to pull continuously and provide change. Otherwise customers may participate only once.

Emphasize the changes by use of window displays and daily advertising and by including the daily specials in major advertising.

CHAPTER

2

Future Lies Ahead: Plan for It

An annual retail calendar, planned well in advance of the next year, can be a great gimmick in successful promotional retailing.

It should be firm enough to show what the store will do in the ensuing months so that at a single glance the retailer can quickly glimpse what lies ahead.

It must be flexible enough to absorb new ideas and events as these may arise.

The calendar itself need not go into detail but it should serve as a guideline to let the retailer know in general what he will be doing and when.

Items to Include in Retail Calendar

BUYING TRIPS

List these as soon as market information is available and dates are set. Preliminary dates can be penciled in early, definite dates inked in later.

ARRIVAL OF MERCHANDISE

Pencil in tentative arrival dates; use a pen for definite dates after confirmation. This will provide a quick resumé of what is arriving, and will be useful in determining dates of promotional activity.

8

EMPLOYEE VACATIONS

Note these on the calendar so they can be taken into consideration when planning promotions.

ANNUAL EVENTS INVOLVING GROUP OR COMMUNITY ACTIVITY

Write these in early so the store's individual promotional calendar can be filled around these major efforts.

Included should be any community activity like the Fourth of July and other seasonal holidays, as well as local festivals and holidays.

SPECIAL DAYS OR WEEKS

These are specifically set aside by federal or state agencies to honor specific people or events. Many lend themselves well to promotions and can involve local facilities, groups, individuals. Included are such items as secretaries, fire prevention, local crops and industries. Lists of these dates are usually available at most newspaper or advertising agencies.

INDIVIDUAL STORE PROMOTIONS

Ink in all traditional annual store promotions; also irregular events such as remodeling sales.

BLANK SPOTS

The remaining blank spots represent areas to be filled in with promotional effort.

Community-Wide Retail Calendar

It is also desirable for the retail group at large to adopt an annual calendar. This should be done early in the fall for the coming year to provide time for individual stores to incorporate joint activities into their calendars and plan accordingly.

Type of Calendar

The type of calendar and its actual physical shape is important only to the retailer; it should suit his individual needs.

Ideas include:

REGULAR CALENDARS

Some may need only a simple ready-made desk calendar, filling in the various activities in the date squares provided.

POCKET-SIZED CALENDARS

Others may prefer to keep a pocket-sized date book or calendar handy at all times. This format is easy to work with if there are a few blank pages in the book where new ideas and notes can be jotted down as they arise.

POSTERBOARD CALENDARS FOR WALL HANGING

Large wall-hanging calendars permit more room for notations and give a full scope at a glance. You can make a good one of posterboard. Map out all the months on a large board (draw your own calendar or paste pages from smaller ones on the posterboard), designing the calendar to fit your wall.

A color-keyed system for elaborate or large operations can be used to make it even more efficient. Use one color to signify "store-only" promotions, another for retail-group events, and a third for national holidays, which are an annual part of the store's retail scene. A fourth can be for community-image or service-oriented efforts.

The colors will indicate if the store is top-heavy in one type promotion or lacking in another.

CHAPTER
3

Good Staff, Better Gimmicks

Employees are powerful and effective elements in the promotional scheme.

They can be invaluable in making customers feel welcome and in building repeat accounts.

So important are employees that any gimmick to increase their effectiveness should be utilized.

Customer Contact

FORMAL CUSTOMER GREETING

Some stores insist clerks walk to the door with customers or that customers be greeted at the door. The formality involved is not necessary unless used with other gimmicks to convey a formal atmosphere.

Employees should, however, greet customers as they see them and make them feel welcome.

ALOOF—BUT AVAILABLE

With today's self-service concept, and with informality a way of life, most customers prefer to shop unhampered by clerks. But they want clerks available so they can ask questions and obtain help. Have clerks master the knack of remaining aloof but readily available.

TELEPHONE CUSTOMERS

Establish a store policy on how clerks are to handle telephone orders. In-store customers resent waiting while clerks serve customers on the phone. This can be avoided in several ways. The usual one is to have the clerk tell the caller that a customer is being served; the clerk should offer to call back or ask the phone customer to wait. If there is a significant number of telephone customers a personal shopper may be needed.

Employee Training

During promotions, employees should know what is going on. Nothing is more frustrating than to ask for an advertised item and have the clerk know nothing about it. Such knowledge is the clerk's business, and it is the retailer's business to make certain every clerk is well informed.

Gimmicks to achieve this include:

At J.C. Penney's, Wash., vacuum cleaners and rug shampoos are demonstrated by specially-trained employees. (Courtesy of Fairchild Visuals)

TRAINING SESSIONS

Hold employee training sessions before events. If changes are made, inform all employees. If the event is long, schedule some training sessions in the middle to keep everyone informed and enthused and to share ideas.

DEPARTMENTAL SESSIONS

Large operations can break these sessions into departmental meetings. Sometimes more can be accomplished in small groups. Even in large stores employees should know what is going on in other departments. If they do, they can refer customers to the proper departments.

SALES-STAFF STIMULATORS

Stimulate salesmanship among the staff, with prizes to those selling the most, breaking a record or meeting a quota.

PLANNING SESSIONS

Include employees in planning sessions. Let them toss out ideas. Hold brainstorming sessions. Encourage employees to talk, regardless of how nutty their idea may be. Inclusion in planning will have the psychological effect of making employees feel important—as though they have a major role in the event.

Employees can also zero in on problems by being able to express their gripes freely, as well as offer what they feel may be customer gripes.

INCLUDE ALL EMPLOYEES

While it is especially desirable to have sales-staff meetings, all other employees should be included in overall general planning sessions. Often the latter do extra work during promotions, receive no extra benefits, and feel left out.

Truck drivers and service men, for example, may come up with ideas and suggestions for their departments and services during promotions or throughout the year; they should get recognition for this. These people have final contact with the customer. Their willingness to make a good lasting impression can spell success or failure in retaining the customer. During promotion, give these employees incentives, too: extra pay or a percentage of the day's volume.

Special training for drivers and servicemen is another gimmick. This should be over and above their technical training and should deal with customer-courtesy.

Part-Time Help

Part-time help is usually a must during holidays and busy periods. For many retailers, this has become a serious problem. Part-time clerks are unfamiliar with the store, merchandise, and methods of operation. Sales can be lost, along with customers, unless part-time help does an efficient job. Some ideas are:

STORE TOURS

Take a tour of the store, giving the part-timer a chance to browse and become familiar with the merchandise. Encourage him to ask for information from regular help when he needs it.

LARGE PRICE LAGS HELP

Unfamiliarity with prices poses problems for part-timers and often results in overpricing or underpricing. Tag items with prices which are large and easily seen.

BUILD A PART-TIME-HELP POOL

If part-time help is needed frequently, build a pool of part-timers. This provides pre-training, knowledge of the store and its operation. Keep lists of full-time employees who leave and who may be available part-time. Use part-time help on a regular basis, calling on the same people whenever possible.

LOCAL SCHOOLS ARE SOURCES

Work with high schools to include a retail course in the curriculum. Students well-trained in retailing will form a pool of part-time employees and be a source of trained full-time help on graduation.

Businessmen can serve as resource people in the classroom and provide time for on-the-job training in the store as part of the retail course. They can supply items at cost to be sold in a school store operated by retailing students.

Night courses for older women or dropouts are a possibility.

If schools refuse to cooperate, retailers can provide training on their own, using nearby college staffs or other professionals to provide non-credit retailing courses for students and adults during evening hours.

COLLEGE STUDENTS

College students usually return at Christmas and during summer months to join the pool of experienced part-time help.

"VOICE OF EXPERIENCE"—BUDDY SYSTEM

Part-timers hesitate to push merchandise the way regular help does. Encourage part-timers to watch regular clerks at work and learn merchandising gimmicks from them. Work out a buddy system with regular employees helping to train extra help.

Store Policy Regarding Employees

Things which may irritate customers should be called to the attention of offending personnel. If necessary, establish a store policy prohibiting offending employee conduct. Among things customers may consider offensive are: social telephone calls which disrupt service; visiting together by employees while a customer waits to be served; rushing a customer who hasn't made up his mind; trying too hard to push an item on an unwilling customer.

CHAPTER
4

Using Credit As
a Promotional Tool

Credit is an essential in retailing today. Customers expect it.

Due to press coverage and governmental controls, most customers are keenly aware that credit costs money. They want it spelled out—and spelled out accurately.

Most stores offer credit under several programs, which is quite a change from the 30-day charge account which began it all.

Among gimmicks involving credit are:

REVERSAL OF "NO CREDIT DURING SALES" POLICY

Reverse this policy and offer credit. Often credit customers feel shunned if they cannot take advantage of low prices during a special event because the promotion and their pay checks do not coincide.

SAVINGS FOR CASH CUSTOMERS

Emphasize the fact that charge cards cost the store a percentage of the sale price, pass the "savings" on to cash customers by giving them a discount. Some credit-card shoppers may change to cash. Some benefits will be that the store will have cash immediately, bookkeeping will be reduced, and the clerks won't be hampered by time-consuming credit-card paperwork.

"Descriptive Billing" lists every charge clearly on a single monthly invoice to help simplify credit transactions.

HONORING CREDIT CARDS

Most customers have them and use them. Many stores now honor more than one. Publicize those accepted in ads, store windows, and in-store displays.

DISCOUNTS FOR TEN-DAY PAYMENTS

Offer small discounts to credit customers who pay statements in ten days. List on the statement the amount which can be deducted, so the customer, seeing it in print, will think of his savings. You might even try a ten-day same-as-cash policy to help get credit accounts paid quickly.

EXTENDED CREDIT WITH NO SERVICE CHARGE

During big promotions or on costly items, offer credit for an extended period, without service charge. Some stores offer it for periods of 30 to 90 days. At Christmas this is becoming traditional, with many stores advertising early in November that customers will have until March 1 or April 1 to pay accounts without a charge being made. Others charge interest only for the 30-, 60-, or 90-day period.

USE LOCAL BANKS FOR CREDIT

For customers who prefer this, arrange financing with a local bank. The finance plan can be written in the store but the bank holds the contract. This eliminates the need of the customer's going to the bank at time of purchase.

An added gimmick is to have payments made at the store. This keeps the store image before the customer, and also may cause him to return, when he will be likely to buy pick-up items. Furthermore, the store knows when the contract is paid off and another large-ticket item can be suggested.

Device between each cashier and customer is a Regiscope which takes simultaneous photo of customer and check—"for your protection" the sign at the extreme left states.

YOUTH CHARGE ACCOUNTS

These are proving highly successful. Parents' permission, in writing, should be a must, but even with this added precaution, retailers should realize the law protects the minor.

Although there are risks involved, the benefits are numerous: customers gained while in pre-teen and teen-age years become loyal customers when they later settle down. They are introduced to the store early and accept it as a shopping center for their needs.

Many have part-time jobs, but saving for a big item is a difficult task. A charge account gives them the item they want, teaches them to take care of their obligations, helps them secure quality, big-ticket merchandise, and instills in them the advantages gained by credit buying if payments are kept up.

Recognize, however, that young people as well as adults, encounter unexpected problems, that emergencies may arise. Tell teen-aged customers that if payments must be missed they should notify the store and make arrangements to make them up.

Parents may want a limit on the amount their child can charge. Note the limit on charge records. Decide with parents if the account is to be for the one item only or if it is to be "open" for the child, so long as the limit isn't exceeded.

SPUR CHARGE SALES

Spur charge sales by sending the charge-account customer a make-believe check for a certain amount. Note on it that his credit is good, and invite him to use the account, adding incentive by offering to redeem the "check" if a stipulated amount of merchandise is purchased by a specific date.

FOLLOW UP INACTIVE ACCOUNTS

Go through all credit accounts and pull those which haven't been used in recent months. Send letters inviting each customer to use the account or providing a special offer as a stimulus to lure the customer back.

CHAPTER

5

The Gift Wrap Helps Sell
the Package

Gift wrapping has become a must—not only at Christmas time but during the other 11 months too. Stores which limit this service to holiday time only may do well to consider expanding the policy.

Gimmicks for this service include:

"TO CHARGE OR NOT TO CHARGE"

Some stores provide free gift wrapping; others charge a small fee. However DON'T LEAVE THE CUSTOMER IN THE DARK. State the policy at the gift-wrap counter. List it on advertising brochures and mailers; on in-store display signs, in ads promoting the service. Such announcements are a must for stores which charge, if they are to avoid customer embarrassment.

FREE AND FEE

Some stores offer free wrapping using an inexpensive wrap and string, but charge for more elaborate wraps. Again—keep the customer informed.

DISPLAY WRAPS OFFERED

Use wall displays showing wraps and bows available, and charges for each. Customers can readily pick out what they want and know immediately what the cost will be.

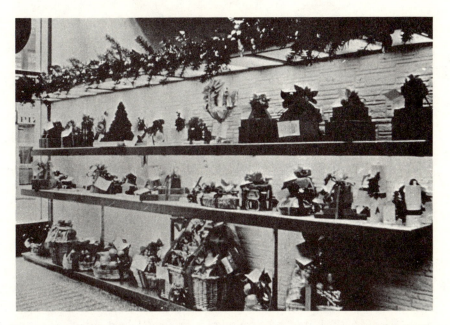

Pre-wrapped gifts can create an interesting wall display. Bloomingdale's, N.Y., did this with holiday and gourmet foods which were wrapped in a traditional manner. (Courtesy of Fairchild Visuals)

FREE BOXES

Many customers prefer to do their own wrapping. But they resent having the gift item slipped into a bag, leaving them to cope with the problem of a box. Post signs at cash registers stating that boxes are available.

GIFT-WRAP COUNTERS

Set up gift-wrap counters to take the burden off sales personnel. Post arrow markers directing customers to the service. Include locations in store directories.

GIFT WRAP CAN BE CONSIDERED A "DEPARTMENT"

Give the service department status. Prevent employee searches for the right-sized box, wrap, bow, or insert tissues while customer lines form by keeping adequate supplies in stock and using an inventory as in other departments. Budget for it. If it must be self-supporting, charge a fee but post it. Allot enough space to do the job adequately; have enough storage shelves and supplies available and a good inventory system worked out so reordering can be done quickly and before items are out of stock.

DECORATED BOXES AND SHOPPING BAGS

Reduce wrapping time and costs by using seasonally decorated boxes and shopping bags, or one elegant box throughout the year, adding seasonal touch by color and type of ribbon used. Highly attractive boxes will not need extra wrapping, unless it is especially requested and charged for.

Gain advertising benefit by using attractive imprinted or embossed stickers, with store name, for attachment to boxes or specially-decorated shopping bags. This adds status to a gift—a touch of exclusiveness.

Offer these boxes free, along with elasticized bow, to customers who will do their own boxing at home.

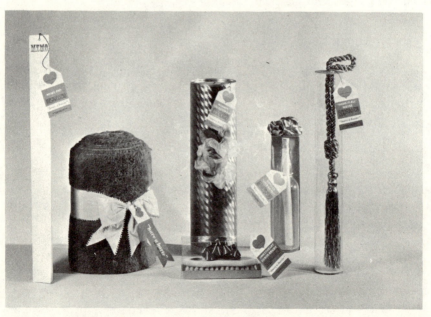

Often inexpensive and unusual gift items can be pre-wrapped in amusing and unorthodox ways. (Courtesy of Harte Creations, Ltd.)

QUICK-SERVICE COUNTER

If long lines form, install a quick-service counter for customers who will accept boxes, and elastic bows. The others will line up at a different counter for more elaborate and time-consuming wraps.

The quick-service counter can have signs indicating that wrapping is simple, that boxes are given for "do-it-yourselfers," that choice of wrap and bow is limited.

Both counters should have signs to advise customers of prices and wraps available at each, so there will be no confusion.

The important aspect is the quick service. The gimmick is to keep the line moving.

QUICK-SERVE SUPPLIES

Use quick-serve supplies. Rolls of paper on cutter-blocks make cutting easier than if clerks fumble with scissors and measuring sticks. Ribbon should be in large rolls, not in small packets. Large piles of tissue for stuffing make packing quick and safe.

ENCLOSURE CARDS

Small gift-enclosure cards and a good pen will be appreciated. The cards may be plain, imprinted with store name only. Or have a small compartmented box of assorted gift-enclosure cards available. A small fee can be charged for these mini-greetings.

MAILER BAGS

For small, flat, unbreakable items, use sturdy mailer-bags. Accordion-like, they lie flat for storage, but an inside panel puffs out for filling. They are strong enough to be suitable for mailing. The gift-wrapped item can be tucked into the bag and mailed (see next chapter on mailing gimmicks), either by the store or customer, depending on service offered. Decorated mailer bags serve a dual purpose—as gift wrap and mailer.

GIFT-WRAPPING CLASSES

Hold gift-wrapping classes in November or early December.

Have a variety of wraps on hand; distribute illustrative booklets from gift-wrap manufacturers.

Many women will do their own wrapping, if they can achieve a professional, creative, personalized result. The classes will probably pay for themselves in reduced requests for the store to do the wrapping. If necessary, make them self-supporting by selling bow-making machines and gift-wrap kits to those participating. Many are available from $1 up.

Conducted properly, the gift-wrapping sessions can become promotional efforts, bringing customers into the store several times. Such classes could be a retail-group project.

GIFT WRAPS FOR MEN AND CHILDREN

Gift-wrapping services are often used by men and children, who aren't adept at wrapping but who want to give impressive gifts.

For children, a nice wrap is all that is required. Let the child watch as his selection is wrapped.

Men, however, appreciate the touch of elegance. If they purchase gifts which are wrapped unattractively, they may have to find another source to rewrap it, making them irritated at the store involved. And their new source could be an enterprising competitor down the street.

One large store reported building goodwill and gaining new customers by wrapping gifts free for men—regardless of where they were purchased.

GIFT-WRAP COUPONS

If a fee is normally charged for elegant wraps, offer the service free as a promotional gimmick during holiday and promotional periods. Or try this on normally slow days.

In ads, you might use coupons which can be redeemed for free gift wrapping on specific days (slow periods) or on specific items.

CHAPTER
6

Mailing Service:
Moving Merchandise Quicker

Mailing service becomes more important as the quick-paced mobile living of the 'seventies continues. Only a few families now are so community oriented that they do not have friends or relatives living elsewhere.

Many women patronize stores especially geared toward mailing services. It's easier; the job is done professionally; there is less chance of breakage; and everything can be handled in one stop. Eliminated are the problems of finding packing boxes, stuffing materials, and address labels and a trip to the post office.

Mailing service, like gift wrapping, is especially important during periods of peak gift buying.

Gimmicks which can be used to promote this service, to offer it quickly and inexpensively, include:

COMBINE WITH GIFT WRAPPING

Combine the mailing counter with the gift-wrap counter. Use envelope-type mailers whenever possible for flat, non-breakable items; the accordion-type envelope mailers, which puff out, are good for large items.

SEPARATE MAILING SERVICE

Some stores may find mailing requires a counter of its own. Shelving and storage area should be provided, along with information slips to be filled out by the customer.

Humor in packaging gifts, particularly when imagination is used, can make items stand out, like this "Investor's Survival Kit" at Saks Fifth Avenue. The "kit" contains party supplies to help you survive a horde of guests. Note the added touch at right of the official "seal." (Courtesy of Fairchild Visuals)

MAIL THE SAME DAY

Customers who want items mailed may assume it will be done promptly. Mail the item the same day as purchase or advise the customer if there will be a delay.

ANNOUNCE AND ADVERTISE SERVICE

Let customers know the service is available. Some stores mail and gift wrap but are secretive about it, hoping the service will be kept to a minimum. This can be a defeatist attitude, as the entire purpose of the gimmick is to provide a service which will generate customers.

STICKY-BACK ADDRESS LABELS

These can cut down on time for both clerk and customer. While the item is being wrapped for mailing, the customer fills in the label, which can be quickly attached to the package. This is better than using information slips, which can be lost or misplaced.

CARD ENCLOSURES

Have gift-card enclosures readily available, along with pen, to be filled in by customers and quickly inserted.

MAILING BOXES

A supply of sturdy, corrugated boxes, stuffing materials, and strong wrapping paper is a must, along with heavy cord. Some customers may be satisfied just to receive these items, wrapping and mailing the item themselves at home.

Or provide counters at the store where the customer can do the actual wrapping, keeping clerks to a minimum, as they will have only to give out the needed materials.

REMOVE TAGS

A must. All mail-counter personnel should be taught to make price-tag removal one of the first steps in serving customers.

HANDLING CHARGES

Most customers won't object to paying a small handling charge for mail service. Departments can actually be made self-supporting by such fees. A scale is needed so postage can be calculated. Most departments charge for this even if the service is free. Postal-rate charts should be readily available.

ZIP-CODE DIRECTORIES

These are needed, too, as many customers don't know zip codes.

SMALL-STORE MAILING SERVICE

A small store need not shun this important service because it is too small to have an individual department.

Regular clerks can handle it. Use address stickers; have customers fill them out. Gifts can then be wrapped at the counter if other customers aren't waiting. Or provide a shelf in a rear room where the items can be stored until clerks can get to them.

CHAPTER

7

Christmas Volume: How to Get It

December—that fast-paced fabulous holiday month—continues as the most important time in the retail calendar. For many, it is the month that can either make or break store volume or profit for the year.

Advertising, promotional efforts, and budgets shift into high gear; new ideas are tried with a dashing air; employees are at an all time high; store doors remain open longer hours; shelves overflow with special items; services like gift wrapping and delivering, often neglected during other periods, come alive; even attitudes and courtesy take on new glitter.

This is the time most stores gain a new image—an entirely new personality.

The activity and accelerated efforts of the Christmas season require early planning. Customers must shop during this period. But there can be no disputing the fact that the gaiety of the shopping district, the overflowing abundance of merchandise, the uniqueness of gimmicks employed by retailers inspire buying far beyond what is necessary to take care of customer shopping-list needs.

One might wonder whether, if the same effort, advertising, expanded budget, and innovative ideas were employed during the other 11 months, those months too might not take on new prominence in store volume and profit.

Gimmicks include:

Twelfth-Month Calendar Gimmicks

STORE PROMOTIONAL CALENDAR

Many stores have found it advantageous to divide the holiday calendar into three categories: early holiday business (Thanksgiving to December 18); last-minute gift buying (December 18 to 24); and the post-Christmas period (after December 26), when easy but time-limited returns are possible, paving the way into next year's activity.

By breaking up the season, promotional efforts can be planned and channeled in the three main directions.

CUSTOMER INFORMATIONAL CALENDARS

Calendars should be used to aid customers by providing them with needed shopping information. These can be used as gimmicks in themselves or as promotional tie-ins.

Calendars in ads should advise store hours and special events like Santa arrivals, Santa visits, and free movies. The newspaper thereby provides printed calendars which customers will keep for reference—if they are complete.

Reminder calendars can be inserted in ads by individual stores as the season progresses.

IN-STORE CALENDARS

Print similar calendars for in-store display and post conspicuously near doors and elevators, and where customers congregate.

YEAR-ROUND CALENDAR CONTESTS

Add a twist to the traditional calendar giveaway by numbering gift calendars consecutively. During the year, pick numbers at random and list several at a time in store windows and advertising. Customers whose calendar numbers are the same as those picked present them at the store for free gifts.

Of prime importance is the type of calendar given—it must be attractive, something a customer will keep and use for a year.

CHARGE-ACCOUNT-CUSTOMER CALENDARS

Advertise a gift-calendar plan for charge customers only. Especially attractive calendars, probably with a coupon-redemption gimmick (see below), are needed to make the idea work. Charge customers receive a calendar by asking for one at the store or by adding to their account, new customers by opening an account.

CALENDAR COUPONS

Calendars can be designed so the page for each month contains a coupon for gift items or discounts if presented at the store. Under this method, all customers receive something. Or sprinkle coupons through the year, making them redeemable quarterly.

CALENDAR COOPERATIVE ADVERTISING

Join with a non-retail firm such as theater or restaurant, gas station or service firm, and make coupons on the store's calendar good for an item at the non-retail firm. The non-retailer gives calendars with coupons good for items at the store. The customer presents the coupon at the place where he got it for validation (stamping), and then presents it to the participating firm for redemption.

This can be done with costs shared between the firms. In this way each firm helps the other build customers.

Christmas Cards

PERSONALIZED CARDS

Add a personal touch by having everyone connected with the store (including truck drivers, office help) sign the card. Time consuming—yes. But in small communities or stores many customers will recognize the personal touch and find the greeting more meaningful.

CARDS WITH GIFTS

Many Christmas cards are now designed complete with small advertising gifts, like pens, rain and hair bonnets, combs, etc. These are always welcome.

Information Booths

These are a real must if confusion is to be avoided. Any busy event raises questions, and holiday time is no exception.

GROUP INFORMATION BOOTHS

Retail-group endeavors can include a central information booth where questions on store hours, specific events, and related matters can be answered.

PUBLIC-SERVICE-ORIENTED BOOTHS

Christmas is the ideal time for retailers to gain community good-will and do some image building by providing other clubs and organizations with help in dispersing their schedules and holiday-activity listings. Churches and civic, religious, women's, school, and other groups can be invited to use the retail information booth for distribution of their schedules and informational flyers.

IN-STORE INFORMATION BOOTHS

Every store can use an information booth of some type. These can advise on store hours and give out gift-suggestion flyers, information on what is available in the various departments, size charts, credit information and even credit application blanks, and information on check-cashing, gift-wrapping, mailing, and delivery services.

TELEPHONE INFORMATION CLEARING HOUSE

A telephone in the store or in the central retail information booth can serve as a clearing house for customers wanting information.

TELEPHONE BOOTHS

A telephone available in the store will be a big help to hurried Christmas shoppers who may have to make personal calls. A similar service should be available at the retailer's central information booth.

Christmas shops can facilitate choosing a gift. A good display can also be built around a Christmas shop. These are wall vignettes to attract people into Christmas shops. (Courtesy of Fairchild Visuals)

ATTRACTIVE INFORMATION BOOTHS

Make information booths appealing and easy to find if they are to serve their purpose.

CHRISTMAS ATTIRE

Green and red ties, smocks, and corsages are simple touches which can add a Christmas touch to the staff manning information booths, even if it's just a regular clerk doing double duty.

Religious Slants

Continued emphasis is placed on the spiritual meaning of Christmas, and there is a real trend away from commercialization of the holiday image. The spiritual side of Christmas can, and should, be incorporated into retail promotional efforts, both in order to avoid criticism and to bring out the real meaning of the holiday.

CHURCH-GROUP PARTICIPATION IN PARADES

Nativity floats are a good idea. So are marching children's choirs. Invite church groups to participate in making floats for the parade, with a separate prize category for religious floats.

NATIVITY SCENES

Urge church groups to provide nativity scenes for public places, even if they are homemade efforts. Store windows may even be made available. This is a good way to fill vacant store windows during the holiday.

BRIEF SPIRITUAL MESSAGES

During Santa visits, especially on his first arrival into the community, or at tree lightings and other Christmas events, have a local clergyman give a brief Christmas spiritual reading.

RELIGIOUS COMMUNITY SINGS

Church groups and choirs should be encouraged to participate in events and lead in community Christmas sings in the business area.

CHURCH BELLS

If there are churches near the retail area, urge them to ring their bells for a few minutes to mark the beginning of the Christmas season. If one has chimes or special bells, brief concerts can be included.

PROVIDE TREATS FOR CHURCH PARTICIPANTS

Youth groups participating in parades and similar activities can be provided hot chocolate or other treats—courtesy of retailers. Women of the church will probably agree to handle the actual work if retailers pick up the tab.

SOUND CAR

Encourage a church group to tour residential and business areas in a sound-equipped car, playing Christmas carols, during the holiday season on several specified evenings. Announcement of retail events or Christmas activities can also be made over the PA system.

CAROLING

Invite church groups to include the retail area in their caroling tours.

Santa's Arrival

Every community traditionally has Santa's arrival to start the season snowballing . . . courtesy of the local retail group. Sparkle and freshness are always desirable and can be achieved by having the jolly old man arrive in varying modes, either alone or at the head of a Christmas parade.

SLEIGH AND REINDEER

Plastic deer and powered sleigh are an idea; or try an old-fashioned sleigh or bobsled pulled by real live horses; or use a float decorated to resemble a sleigh if a parade is held.

COVERED WAGON

Go "Old West," and make a covered wagon garnished with holly and Christmas greens.

MILITARY VEHICLES

Communities near military installations are often able to use military vehicles. Have Santa arrive by helicopter, come down the river on a barge, or steam in on a Coast Guard cutter, perhaps even drive in by tank or jeep. Return the favor by having Santa visit the base, appearing at programs scheduled there.

LAND AND SEA

Airports and the area around rivers make good landing spots and can usually accommodate large crowds if arrangements are made in advance.

FIRE TRUCKS

Every community has one; if there is a vintage truck which is the pride of the department, toot that out for the occasion.

DO IT UP DIFFERENTLY

One Texas community used a calliope. With imagination you might employ things in the community such as huge farm vehicles, snowmobiles, or dune buggies; or even a vintage vehicle an area collector might have.

DEPOTS

Even if train service has long since stopped, many communities have engines in their railroad yards which can be utilized for a short haul. Many railroads will cooperate. Old depots also make good headquarters for Santa, especially if trains are used for his arrival.

TRY WALKING

If Santa is young and vigorous, let him try walking. How about a hike in on snowshoes?

UNSEASONAL APPROACHES

Consider having Santa arrive on a power lawnmower, pulling a small tractor—full of candy canes which can be tossed to children along the route by helping elves.

DECORATE SANTA'S ROUTE

Perk up the parade route, if possible, with a theme (you could make it candy-cane lane) or use garlands, trims, pole decorations.

Tree-Lighting Ceremony

Next to Santa's visit, the tree-lighting ceremony ranks highest as a traditional event. The official lighting of the huge community

Outdoor decorations play an important role, especially during the Christmas holidays. (Courtesy of Fairchild Visuals)

tree can be combined with Santa's parade, his arrival, or even a later visit.

Regardless of what is included, make the ceremony something to remember. Here are some ideas:

SYNCHRONIZED LIGHTING

Synchronize Santa's watch and that of a city switchman so that at a given signal Santa can wave his magic wand (candy cane will do) and the lights appear. Of course, have Santa ready to ad-lib in event timing goes astray. A few extra waves can add intrigue and take up needed time if the gremlins foul things up.

RELIGIOUS PARTICIPATION

Tree-lighting ceremonies lend themselves to religious readings or group sings as a method of beginning or ending them.

COORDINATE MUSICAL AND LIGHTING EQUIPMENT

Synchronize sound equipment to the tree's lighting. Available at cost ranging from several hundred to several thousand dollars (depending on how elaborate you want things), tape recorders can be synchronized to tree lights. Special equipment will make soft colored lights sparkle during times when soft notes are played. As music increases in tempo and intensity, lights darken. Once hooked up, the equipment is automatic and can run through the holiday period with no trouble. This is a tremendous drawing card for out-of-town tourists; it is especially nice if there is a plaza or walk where spectators can stay to watch and listen.

SANTA'S-HELPER CONTESTS

Tree lighting lends itself to contests. How about one where a child's name is drawn from those deposited in participating stores before the holiday season opens? He becomes Santa's official helper or "Brownie" for the ceremony (or the balance of the season). Give him a simple costume, red cape with white fur trim, and include him in Christmas activities.

Santa Visits

In most communities Santa visits several times. There is no end to ways these can be treated to stir interest. Ideas include:

RETAIL-GROUP SANTA HEADQUARTERS

Some groups may find it desirable to build a centrally located headquarters for Santa or to find him one (old depot, unused building, theater lobby, etc.). All retailers benefit and share cost.

SANTA STATIONERY

In a group venture, give out Santa stationery in participating stores. Children deposit their Santa letters at the central Santa headquarters, and a mass-produced reply is sent them.

LUNCH WITH SANTA

Tie in with a local women's club and use a central location. Provide simple lunches for all children; keep the fee small, if one must be charged. Sandwiches, carrot and celery sticks, potato chips, milk, and Christmas cookies are ample.

Santa arrives and eats with the children, after which he visits individually, hearing requests.

SANTA PHOTOS

Cover the cost of Santa visits or lunches by selling photos of Santa with the child as they visit. Use commercial firms to handle photography or man someone with Polaroid, so parents can get an instant photo which is paid for on the spot. A $1 fee per Polaroid picture will help defray costs.

SANTA STORY HOURS

Very simple—instead of having Santa visit with each child, have him and/or Mrs. Claus read to the children, keeping them all amused while parents shop.

SANTA HOUSES

Something unusual in Santa houses can be provided easily and inexpensively. Turn a drab in-store Santa corner into a real headquarters by giving it a theme: try a gingerbread house, with Mrs. Claus on hand to help (give out gingerbread men to little guests); a gigantic velvet throne; a workshop for Santa and his helpers; a North Pole house; or maybe a sleigh from which Santa can give out candy and chat with tots.

Child-Sitting Services

Among ideas which can be used to amuse small children while parents shop are:

FREE MOVIES

Arrange with local theaters for matinees while parents shop. Or set up home-movie projectors in individual stores for a mini-theater

Many stores can use a joint advertisement to announce Santa's arrival, free movies, other Christmas activities—and store hours.

approach. Go all out and provide free popcorn and comics; remember to allow for frequent stretch periods if small fry are to remain content.

POST BEGINNING AND ENDING TIMES

Avoid confusion and despair by posting beginning and ending times so no child is left stranded after free entertainment ends.

THEATER CHRISTMAS PARTY

If movies are provided at a local theater, arrange with a restaurant or woman's organization to provide inexpensive family snacks afterward. These will free mom from having to rush home and prepare a meal, and give the entire family a chance to continue shopping.

PUPPET SHOWS

Use local or professional talent for this all-time favorite.

AFTERNOON MATINEE FOR PRE-SCHOOLERS

Include an afternoon matinee or other form of entertainment for pre-schoolers so mom can shop alone while older children are still at school and when stores are not crowded.

BABY-SITTING SERVICE

Some stores may want to provide their own. A small nook and a supply of pencils, paper, blunt-edged scissors, paints, and similar items are all that's needed. Eliminate chairs by using a large rug; most tots prefer the floor level. A color television will help amuse small fry.

A woman employed as Mrs. Claus can man the center. Maybe a nursery school approach, with retired kindergarten teachers as staff, will do.

For last-minute shopping, offer in-store baby-sitting the week before Christmas. Many students are out of school at this time and can be employed.

RECORDING OR FILM STUDIO

Turn the baby-sitting service into something for which the kids will really love you—and remember. Make recordings of Santa talking with them. In later years these can be played over loudspeakers to "crack up" adults in future promotional efforts.

Or film the children and file away the prints for later viewing. Run the film in a store window or inside the store some hot summer day, long after the holiday has passed, for a CHRISTMAS IN JULY approach.

REMOTE TV

Use this device and the child will see himself on the screen while talking to Santa or while being cared for. This will hold interest for a long time.

KEEP IT COMFORTABLE

Avoid complicated things which are hard to cope with on a group basis. If treats are provided, stay away from hard sticky candy, which bring up hand-washing problems and the possibility of choking. Cookies are great. Rugs are better than chairs, which are bound to tip over.

SANTA TELEPHONES

Instead of supervised baby-sitting, scatter the service through the store so tots can be amused nearby while mom shops: install fake phones at a low level which play a recorded message from Santa after S-A-N-T-A is dialed.

IMPROMPTU BABY-SITTING AREAS

Scatter a few sets of small tables and chairs about the store where children can sit and color while mom shops at nearby counters. Or use small television sets and a rug for a TV area. Parents themselves are responsible for children left at these informal centers.

SLEIGH RIDES

These are popular again and can be arranged on a retail-group basis. Have trips of 45 minutes' duration, giving parents that much time to shop while children are amused on the trip. This will eliminate need for in-store nursery areas.

Have older teens or adults along to insure safety of little ones. Also, check insurance to make certain there is adequate coverage.

Children's Shopping Hours

A number of gimmicks can be used to make children's shopping hours easy on mom and child. They are:

SUPERVISION

If a child is left in a designated area to shop, clerks should watch him until his mom retrieves him.

SANTA'S HELPERS

Clerk assistance in helping the child with his selection will be appreciated. Turn clerks into Santa's helpers.

LOW TABLES AND DISPLAYS

Put merchandise suitable for gift giving on low tables in a separate section of the store. Restrict traffic in this spot to children only and have clerks on hand to assist youngsters and supervise them so they are never alone.

PRICE RANGES IMPORTANT

Have merchandise in the 50¢-to-$1 range in one section, and that from 10 to 50 cents in another, so children can be grouped around tables suited to their budgets.

CHILDREN ONLY

Insist that parents refrain from accompanying the child into the restricted area. This is not fair to their child or the other children, who want the privilege of shopping alone.

If necessary, provide a pot of coffee along with a few chairs for anxious parents who insist on lingering nearby.

GIFT-SELECTION LISTINGS

List gift selections available in the various price brackets and give these printed lists to parents when they leave their children. Parents fill in the list and leave it with the child. Clerks use these as a guideline in assisting young buyers.

Or print the listings in advertisements beforehand so they can be clipped, filled in, and sent with the child.

TREAT LITTLE SHOPPERS

Have a buffet area where milk and cookies await. Or give each child a candy cane as he leaves.

GIFT WRAPPING

Keep it simple—BUT DO IT. This can be the finishing touch to a memorable event. It will also insure the tyke's gift will be kept secret from prying older brothers and sisters. Provide small gift tags and attach to each gift so the child doesn't get them confused by the time he gets home.

Stag Nights

Just as children need special attention, so do husbands, dads, and lads.

Stag nights are almost as traditional as the old whiskered man himself, having proven highly popular in recent years.

The gimmick is to make the event strictly stag. Try these ideas:

OPEN SHOP ONE EXTRA NIGHT

Insert one extra night opening in the calendar; make it "men only" and then promote around it.

ROPE OFF A SECTION

Rope off one section as the Stag Center, either for a specific night or for the entire season.

REFRESHMENTS

Coffee and donuts will do; but some retailers use this as the time to say "thanks" to the men, so they include fancy buffets and cocktails.

SPECIFIC HOURS

Set definite hours if the event is to be a one-night stand; you might include a program of entertainment, and run it till midnight.

APPAREL SHOWS

Girl models show enticing fashions for ladies on the men's gift lists.

DEMOS

Sports, workshop, and hobby equipment, electrical appliances— these are all items men like to buy. Demonstrations by professionals are good.

MERCHANDISE LISTINGS

Listings can be printed in ads so mom can give an assist before the big night by marking off items she and the youngsters especially want.

SIZE CHARTS

Include in advertisements of stag affairs so mom can mark sizes down first rather than having hubby "guesstimate" later. Or give wallet-sized gift-list or size charts to women customers beforehand, so men will have them readily available when they shop.

Correct sizes mean fewer returns. Investment in wallet-type size charts can be profitable by eliminating such returns. Keep them on hand year around and get customers in the habit of using them.

GIVEAWAYS TO TAKE HOME

Take-home gifts are always nice, especially if they are something the man can take home to the lady on his list: boxed mistletoe; small decorated trees or corsages, bow-making kits, perfume samples, hankies. For the women to give to men, try Christmasy bow-ties, pens, key chains, matches, calendars, and pocket combs.

Gals Only

It was only natural that from stag night a "gals only" night should evolve. Long before women's lib became fashionable, women appreciated the opportunity to shop alone and be catered to. So stage a ladies-only promotion, insisting women shop alone and not drag husband or children along.

FASHION SHOWS

Use children, high-school students, and college students to model garments which will be on their shopping lists. College boys are ideal for men's garments, and this will add a new twist to the traditional retail fashion show for women.

REFRESHMENTS

A must for the gals. Coffee breaks should include rolls or tea sandwiches, diet specials.

PRICING

Racks and tables listing price brackets of special merchandise will make shopping easy.

TAKE-HOME GIFTS

Any little memento will do—the list is endless. Advertising or sample specialties with a Christmas touch are good.

DEMONSTRATIONS

Again, these are good. Any type of item can be demonstrated, from games for children to outboard motors.

Stag and Drag

Well—why not?

Let stags drag their gals to a co-ordinated event for couples only.

Cooperate with other stores to add real appeal. A store catering to men can hold a Stag Night while a store for women holds a Ladies' Night, with the final gimmick being joint coffee, a buffet, or entertainment afterward, sponsored by the two outlets.

A large store can do a Stag-and-Drag promotion alone, segregating his and her shopping areas and staging a joint coffee/entertainment later.

Christmas Cookie, Cake, and Candy Capers

These can range from baking events to recipe swapping. Endless gimmicks can be built around them; try one of these.

WOMEN'S CLUB TIE-IN

Work with a woman's organization which wants to earn money by having a cookie-and-coffee break one morning. Tables are set in one area to permit women to display cookies. The gals may have their recipes typed on cards beforehand, to be sold individually. Or the recipes may be bound into cookbooks for sale.

Cookies, too, can be sold individually with a cup of coffee to be consumed on the spot, as well as by the dozen or pound.

Invite workers in the shopping area—as well as customers—to use the event for their morning coffee break.

The women's group should handle this themselves—the store merely suggests the idea and makes space available.

CHRISTMAS COOKIE TREE

Let employees or customers bring in cookies they have decorated to hang on the store tree. Contests can be staged and prizes given.

COOKIE-TREE TREATS

Have a commercial bakery made cookies in Christmas shapes, and put each in a plastic bag. Hang on the store tree to give to little folks; replenish the tree ornaments daily with more from the bakery.

DECORATING PARTIES

These can revolve around cake and cookie decoration, which can be demonstrated easily in stores.

Contests can be developed, with some of the decorated items given as prizes (or the instructor may bake some highly decorated item beforehand to be given as prizes). Or have a pot of coffee on and let customers at the demonstration eat 'em all up.

RECIPE CONTESTS

These can work in a number of ways. Either recipes or actual baked goods may be entered. Home economists with school or extension programs can judge. Recipes entered can be mimeographed and given to contestants, or they can be bound into booklet form and sold later.

Turn the event into an old-fashioned fair and have entrants submit actual baked items, with judges sampling each. The items, minus sample slice can be sold, with profits going to a local Christmas charity program. Or the entire assortment may be given as a grand prize to the winner. Or, after the sampling, all the goodies may be taken to a local children's home, thereby gaining publicity for the store. Still another idea is to invite the public, men included, to stop by, and then to hold an auction as a means of selling the items, giving the money to a local charity for a Christmas program.

Christmas Safety

Emphasize Christmas safety in numerous ways including:

LOCAL RESOURCE PEOPLE

Have demonstrations using nearby college staff, local police and fire chiefs to stress safety in products sold.

DEMOS

Have demonstrations on how to fireproof a tree or how to make fire-retardant Christmas decorations; discuss safe tree lighting and decorating techniques; include candles and their proper use during holiday periods as a topic.

Hold workshop sessions to stress safety. One idea is to use battery-operated candles for displays and to encourage their use in homes, at children's pageants and plays. Keeping adequate water in tree stands; keeping trees away from heat sources; not blocking exits with trees; proper disposal of trees; how to keep them from tipping over are all good things to stress in such a workshop.

Show spectators how to turn a used Christmas tree into a tree from which food for birds can be hung, prolonging its usefulness and helping wildlife too. Conservationists can give that type of demonstration.

Flameproofing of clothing (which can be handled by home economists) and cleaning operations (there are always spills at holiday time) are good workshop ideas.

Trading Stamps

These can be used to promote the holidays; ideas include:
DOUBLE- AND TRIPLE-STAMP DAYS
Spur business on dull days with these time-proven promotions.
EXTRA STAMPS
Push Christmas merchandise by giving added stamps on items which are moving slow.

LOCAL TIE-IN

If a group is collecting stamps for a specific item like a kidney machine and thousands of books are needed, hold a triple-stamp day. But insist that customers deposit stamps in a container which will be turned over to the group. Customers who wish to retain stamps receive only the normal amount. This is a good way to pull many women from affiliated clubs on normally slower days.

STAMP-BOOK SWAP

This is always going on, but the tempo increases at holiday time. Help customers with their stamp trading by setting aside a bulletin-board area where customers can list books they have to trade and which ones they want. Or hold a swapping party right in the store at a specific time.

Christmas Baby

Get the jump on the traditional New Year's Baby contest or give the entire thing a new twist by switching to a Christmas baby.

CHRISTMAS BABY

The baby born first on Christmas Day or thereafter receives a surprise visit from Santa—right in the hospital at mom's bedside. Let the jolly old man bear the gifts and present them right there.

STOCKINGS FOR BABY

Send Christmas babies home from the local hospital in bright red stockings, courtesy of the retail group. These must be oversized, large enough to hold a blanket-wrapped baby. A local seamstress will be able to make them up.

Rudolph and His Friends

Rudolph and his friends continue to fascinate wee folk—and their parents too. Use them wherever deer will fit into the scheme of things, or try these ideas designed specifically for them.

WINDOW DECORATIONS

Use a sleigh, complete with red-nosed Rudolph, and have a contest to determine how often his nose blinks in an hour, a day, or during the holiday season.

FIND RUDOLPH

Have Rudolph conspicuously missing from window or in-store display and offer prizes to the person who finds him. He could be hidden somewhere in the store, or in the community at large if a retail group is involved in the promotion. Build interest by giving out tips each day on where he may be lurking.

LIVE DEER

These are always good and can be obtained from private promotional agencies for holiday use.

Lighting Contests

These continue to grow in popularity, with numerous gimmicks possible as offshoots from these basic ideas:

HOME-LIGHTING CONTEST

This encourages residents to decorate homes and yards, with retailers giving prizes for the best displays. Break into two categories: regular lighting and religious themes.

HOW MANY LIGHTS?

Give prizes for the person guessing the correct number of lights on in-store or community Christmas tree.

LIGHTING CLASSES

Bring in experts from lighting firms and power companies to give out tips and ideas early in November on yard and house lighting.

Last-Minute Shoppers

Gift certificates are probably the most popular item for chronic last-minute shoppers. They have become old stand-bys, but they aren't too imaginative. The retailer who comes up with a cute last-minute-shopping Christmas suggestion will attract the customer who is still looking.

Here are some ideas which can be used as bait for these people:

GIFT LISTS

Publish gift lists at the last minute specifically for them, including novel ideas and varied prices. Post similar listings in the store where they can be referred to readily.

LAST-MINUTE-SHOPPERS' TABLE

This type of customer does not like to shop. Use special tables or counters, and keep them stocked with a wide variety of items for last-minute shoppers. Have one clerk keep an eye on the table in case help is needed, but generally help should remain aloof. These people like to get their shopping over with, selecting an item without great consultation.

GIFT WRAPPING

This is a must. These customers dislike wrapping even more than shopping. Quick wrapping can be provided by the clerk

manning the last-minute-shoppers' table. Size charts should also
be readily available for reference.

Last-Minute Pick-Up Gifts

Every family has this problem and it can begin early in the
week before Christmas when a gift for the Sunday School pageant
is needed or when mom realizes teacher has been forgotten and
tomorrow is the last day of school.

Momentum gains until late Christmas Eve—that magical time
when memories start clicking on.

Ideas to serve these needs include:

LOW-PRICED PICK-UP TABLE

Keep a table close to the door with merchandise in low price
ranges. People don't usually forget those who will receive major
items.

ADVERTISE

Let customers know you have a special pick-up table; promote
this gimmick right up until the store closes.

STAY OPEN LATE CHRISTMAS EVE

At least one store should stay open. This can be done on a
group basis, with retailers pooling merchandise so a selection is
available at a central location where a late Christmas Eve last-
minute-shoppers' counter is available.

Items to include are tree lights, tinsel, gift wraps, ribbons,
pick-up gifts, cards, lower priced gift items for male and female
in all age groups.

College Students

Remember this group—they can be of real impact on the
volume side of the ledger if they are catered to.

Many wait until they return home to shop rather than hauling bulky gifts back with them. Most will arrive several days before Christmas—when things are getting hectic—so they will appreciate promotions geared towards them.

COLLEGE NIGHT

Give students their own night, similar to stag or ladies' night affairs.

''WELCOME HOME'' PARTY

Toss a real "welcome home," giving college students the run of the store for one evening. Combine with refreshment bar where they can meet old friends. Records can provide atmosphere and background music.

Fashion shows, demonstrations, and special buys will entice them.

Provide ample time for browsing, selecting, and visiting.

Miscellaneous Christmas Ideas

HELLO SANTA

Recruit Santas from among the men's civic, service, and religious groups and hold a "Santa Speaking" or "Hello Santa" night. Have as many trunk lines put into the store as needed, with the pool of Santas manning the phones from 6 to 8 p.m. on a specified night or nights. Children can call in and personally chat with Santa during that period.

SANTA SUITS FOR PUBLIC USE

Every store or retail group eventually has a Santa suit which has become shabby. Make it available at no charge to residents for at-home Christmas parties or to area groups and organizations.

MAKE CHRISTMAS STORIES COME ALIVE

One large Minneapolis store spent two years, considerable research, and a sizeable investment to unfold a "Dickens' Village"

Reprinting an ad that appeared 44 years earlier draws attention to the Christmas parade. A touch of the past is always a good promotional gimmick.

for its customers. All the people and places of the famed author's stories came alive with 150 almost life-sized characters, many of them animated, shown living and working in the village.

Elaborate displays like this can be staged, even by smaller stores (admittedly on a smaller scale), with stores adding new characters and pieces each year. Or let the retail group get together and use the same theme in all stores to provide a unified Christmas effect.

SENIOR CITIZENS ENJOY CHRISTMAS TOO

Remember the customers of yesteryear. Special shopping hours just for them can be arranged. Have a women's club provide members to help the older people with their shopping. Use men from service clubs and religious groups to provide transportation for the senior citizens from nursing homes to downtown areas.

Get youth in on the act by having them carol and lead the older shoppers in a community sing.

Bring in Santa to visit and chat with the older folks.

Don't forget snacks and gifts.

Remember those who are too old or too ill to participate by having Santa visit area nursing homes, accompanied by youthful carolers, bearing token gifts and treats.

REMEMBER THE ILL

Similar visits and promotional efforts can be geared toward the ill in hospitals and convalescent homes.

CHRISTMAS AND NATURE

Everyone is talking about nature and ecology; these can be tied in nicely with the Christmas season. Have a nature tree, with ornaments made of pine cones, dried weeds, and other such things. Work through schools, with children providing the ornaments.

Sponsor workshops geared toward making Christmas wreaths and decorations from weeds, pine cones, boughs, and other nature items.

Stress use of leftover trees and the role they can play in providing shelters for wildlife. Youth groups might be interested in working at a Christmas-oriented nature project, and many will come up with novel ideas.

REMEMBER THE ANIMALS

Humane groups are always anxious to work on promotional efforts geared toward finding homes for stray cats and dogs. Use publicity to highlight the animals at the shelter and that they would make good pets for some child on Christmas morning. Or hold a promotion in the store, with a percentage of the sales going to the shelter, and urge residents to remember the shelter in their Christmas donations.

CHRISTMAS CLUB

Christmas club checks mean sales. Offer a bonus to customers who convert their club checks into merchandise certificates. A $100 check would mean $105 or $110 in merchandise certificates.

Converting the entire check is one idea. But this can lose potential "converters", if the club check is big and they do not want to spend it all in one store. A certain amount, therefore, can also be offered to those who convert only a portion of each check.

SANTA'S HELPERS

Be a Santa's helper and aid customers with their shopping by having them save sales slips for a specified period before the holiday season, or early in the holiday period, perhaps Thanksgiving to December 15. The person presenting the largest amount gets a bonus certificate to be redeemed for merchandise; or give all customers merchandise certificates based on a percentage of their sales slips.

GIFT CERTIFICATES

These are especially good for the opening of the season if done on a retail-group basis.

Each store gives one during opening festivities. Or they can be printed in ads and redeemed at the stores by specific dates.

Early sales can be spurred by stipulating that the certificate be redeemed within a given time. This starts customers shopping locally at the beginning of the season when stock is complete.

GROUP COUPON PROMOTIONS

These are successful when staged by groups of retailers midway between opening and end of season, when things tend to lag. It must be planned in advance and ready to be put into use when the need arises.

All participants run ads on the same day; each bears a coupon with the store's name. These highlight one item that is greatly reduced at each store. Coupons must be turned in when making the purchase.

The vast array of merchandise available at great savings has great drawing power.

Add a novel twist by allowing space on the coupons for names and addresses, so these can be placed in boxes in the stores for a drawing to be held later.

BONUS CHRISTMAS SALE

Offer a percentage of the total sales as a bonus on merchandise sold during a stipulated number of days, giving the customer his choice of anything priced at that amount in the store. The bonus is often applied by customers on higher priced items with the result that big ticket merchandise is moved.

BREAKFAST WITH SANTA—FOR ADULTS

Adults like Santa too. Spur early morning traffic by holding breakfasts with Santa on normally dull days. If necessary, limit group size by giving out tickets beforehand. Keep menus simple: orange juice, sweet buns, fancy coffee cakes, beverages are all easy for in-store serving. Limit the affair to a half-hour or so, with Santa giving out token gifts.

These are usually for women only, and may include mini-fashion shows featuring holiday gift items, decorating ideas, the latest in table settings for holiday dining. This is an excellent time for quickie showings of new Christmas merchandise. If an item is unique, pass it around for inspection. For a prize, women write down birthdays; the one closest to December 25 wins.

End events like this with a group sing—"Jingle Bells" is always good.

BRUNCH WITH SANTA

Brunch—lunch—call it what you want. Follow the breakfast promotion outlined above.

BOX-DAY PROMOTION

Brighten things up midway through the holidays by staging a Box Day. Pre-boxed merchandise will be used to lure customers in, with a small discount on specific items the incentive.

SANTA'S BAG CONTEST

Use a local site like a bank lobby as the place to locate a Santa figure or have it in an individual store. Use a Santa with a huge bag; ask customers to register for giveaway presents. Let this cover a six- to eight-week period, spurring interest by removing the entries each week and choosing ten or 12 as potential winners, with the grand winner to be selected from among them. Post and publicize names of weekly winners who are still in the running to draw interest, giving the grand prize on Christmas eve at the end of the retail selling season.

WISHING WELL

Build a wishing well of cardboard or plywood; customers put entry slips in stating their wish (within stipulated price range). Winner is determined by drawing.

GIFT STOCKING

Order in a supply of red Christmas stockings (or have them made locally) and use to hold gifts. Make a nominal charge for the unique wraps, and advertise by saying the stocking wraps are something any proud Santa would leave hanging over a fireplace on Christmas eve.

You might do it around St. Nicholas' Day (December 6), as many families observe the ancient custom of hanging stockings filled with oranges, candy, and cookies on St. Nicholas' Eve. If the custom isn't observed in the community, retailers can start it as an added holiday attraction.

DECEMBER DOLLAR DAYS

Many retailers eliminate monthly Dollar Day activity during December. Reverse this policy and feature one, early in the month. The event may pull more than it does at other times, and it will help reduce inventory and stock so efforts can be concentrated more heavily on Christmas selling.

SHOPPERS' CHRISTMAS EXPRESS

Use specially decorated cars or buses in outlying suburban areas to bring customers in for specific shopping hours or special events. Decorate the vehicles in green or red, or have one resembling an oversized sleigh.

If there are a number of outlying areas, feature a shoppers' express to various ones on specific days, with banners in store windows greeting customers from the area served.

CHRISTMAS MESSAGE CONTEST

Telephone calls to loved ones are appreciated and make ideal prizes during Christmas contests.

GIFT-ARAMA

Boost sales of big ticket items by allowing customers who purchase these to choose a gift from a selection of lower priced merchandise. Aluminum trees, unusual lighting or tree decorations are good.

Christmas Returns

Returned merchandise can become a real headache if definite policies aren't established—and advertised beforehand. Often this is best done on a retail-group basis, to take pressure off individual retailers.

Keep in mind the policy must be firm to be effective; but the good will of customers is also a must. There will be some who really can't return gifts by specified dates (vacations, funerals, illness are among valid reasons).

Advertise immediately before Christmas what the return policy will be. Keep the policy posted in store windows and in ads immediately after Christmas. State that returns will be welcome during a specific period (and smile, during that period, at customers returning merchandise). January 1 is usually a preferred cutoff date. Use bold, dark type and specify no returns after that date.

Even exchange days can have a novel gimmick or twist. Be the most talked-about store in town by advertising credit will be given toward any unwanted gift regardless of where it was purchased. The gimmick is that the credit must be used to purchase ·something in your store. This will spur traffic and cause excitement if the returned items are later auctioned off. Profit can be retained by the store or given to a local charity or project.

Christmas Clearance

Leftover Christmas stock can be cleared immediately after the holidays instead of left on shelves far into January, if imagination is used.

EARLY STORE HOURS

Attract bargain seekers the day after Christmas with large markdowns. Try a daybreak sale starting at 7 a.m., serving coffee and rolls to bring customers in early.

CLEARANCE AUCTION

Number items to be cleared; stock on a separate table or in store window; let customers bid on them from December 26 through the end of the week. Hold an auction the day after New Year's, with the highest bidder receiving the item. Or hold the bidding on New Year's Day for a gala affair.

Add excitement by making it a retail-group event, with retailers assembling leftover merchandise at a central location, where it can be inspected and bids submitted, winding it up on New Year's Day. A code-numbering system can be used on the items so each store receives credit for his merchandise sold. Or just hold an auction to get rid of the leftovers with no pre-bidding.

CHRISTMAS IN JULY

If storage space is available, bundle up leftover stock immediately after Christmas and pack it away for a July promotion. Mark down the items then to the same prices at which they would have been sold if the clearance had been held after the holiday.

A real promotional effort can be built around this during the warm days of summer. Santa could even make an appearance; Christmas cookies could be served and a tree set up.

CHAPTER
8

Other Special Occasions

Holidays, birthdays, anniversaries, and other special occasions are supreme times for promotional activity. Novel gimmicks, simple sales, or a "thank you" to customers for shopping and adding to the store growth are all factors which can be woven into these events.

Birthday-Anniversary Ideas

These are ideal times to say, "Tank you," to customers who have helped make growth possible since the store was founded. They are also the times to invite new customers in.

Try these to build birthday parties around:

OLD MONEY

Coins lend themselves to many adaptations. If the store was 20 years old in 1970, for example, gifts could have been given to customers offering coins dated 1950—the year the store opened. Gifts could have been of varying values, to go with pennies, nickels, dimes, etc.

Or focus on bills, using the serial number as the basis. For example: number B7192059 is a winner because the numerals "2" and "0" appear in the bill in the right order. You might urge customers to try for a serial number that bears the entire store opening

Retailers in Norfolk, Va., sponsored a Cultural Festival through the Chamber of Commerce. Painting and sculpture exhibits, concerts, plays and puppet shows were all featured. (Courtesy of Associated Visual Arts Studio, Norfolk, Va.)

date; e.g., B1195023. The approach is to redeem the coin or bill to get it out of circulation so it can't be redeemed twice.

Spur real interest by giving a grand award to the person who turns in the most coins during the event.

ANTIQUES AND OLD ITEMS

These also lend themselves to birthday celebrations. Use displays of items manufactured or sold during the period when the store was young.

Old newspaper clippings are good items around which to build displays and promotions. Try a "remember when" theme, highlighting events that happened in the year the store opened.

Give prizes to customers who bring in items dated with the same year, such as old fruit jars. Many such items are dated. Stir enthusiasm by using these in the window along with name cards.

Include photos of the really unusual items in ads, along with pictures of customers owning the items. Many of these may be heirlooms, so precautions should be taken to insure their safety while on display.

BIRTHDAY-GREETING DISCOUNT CERTIFICATES

Give discount certificates or gifts to customers who celebrate their birthdays during the same month the store does.

BIRTHDAY CAKES

If it is difficult to serve cake slices, try cupcakes and coffee.

Novel birthday cake ideas include baking coins inside of them, or in capsules in which gift certificate numbers are included. If the store is 50 years old, include 50 coins or capsules in the cake. Have only one capsule contain a number corresponding to the age of the store; the person who receives that slice of cake redeems the capsule for a prize.

BIRTHDAY PUNCHBOARD

Use a giant punchboard; for every $5 spent, the customer can punch out a number. Winners are those whose numbers correspond to the birthday number. If the store is 66 years old, numbers ending or beginning in six win, with the grand prize to the number 66.

JOINT BIRTHDAY CELEBRATIONS

If several stores celebrate birthdays during the same year, team up and make it a joint celebration. Advertise together, offer specials during specific hours, and hold joint contests.

ANNIVERSARY COUPLES

Use the word "anniversary" instead of "birthday" and you have an entirely new slant on things. Example: hold similar contests but use anniversaries instead of birthdays as the basis, with couples celebrating anniversaries the same month being winners. Oldest couple celebrating an anniversary during the month can be grand winner. Giveaway items can include decorated anniversary cakes.

BIRTHDAY CAKE WITH WOMEN'S CLUB TIE-IN

Co-ordinate activity with a women's club desiring to hold a bake sale. The store agrees to buy some of the best decorated cakes members bring in. These can be served with free coffee by the store. It will help add stimulus to store activity and to the bake sale.

BIRTHDAY MARKDOWNS

Mark down prices on specific items, or special order in items that lend themselves to birthday promotions. Price the specials to correspond to age of the store or year it opened. If it is 20 years old, prices could range from 20 cents up to dollar amounts ending in 20; e.g., $19.20.

Use a "remember when prices were this low" theme to highlight the bargains.

FAMOUS PERSON TIE-IN

Do some historic research and determine what famous persons would have celebrated birthdays on the same date. Build promotional efforts around these.

PREDICT THE FUTURE

Look ahead to the future and do something now that can be used as the basis for future promotions. Example: hold a "looking ahead" promotion, and let customers write down their predictions on what the store or city will be like five or ten years hence. Bury these in a birthday ceremony and advertise that they will be dug up five or ten years later. Use pictures and gain publicity now and again in the future.

New Year's Day

Another great day—the only time to launch an entirely new year.

BREAK WITH TRADITION AND STAY OPEN

Most stores continue to close on New Year's Day, but there are events that lend themselves to remaining open. These do not have to be geared to actual selling—they can be a celebration or community service promotion.

Entertain customers by having them in for a New Year's brunch; to watch the ball game on color TV. Or use an open-house approach, giving customers a chance to browse around, visit, enjoy a snack; but advertise no sales will be made, and stick to the policy.

GIGANTIC NEW YEAR'S CLEARANCE

Do something really different. Open the store and sell. Hold a gigantic New Year's Day clearance sale. Or begin on New Year's Eve, combining the sale with a party, with special gifts for those who are still there as the New Year dawns.

RESOLUTIONS

Capitalize on "resolutions," and hold a contest for the most original; the most ridiculous; most humanitarian; the resolution most likely to succeed. Or have customers enter their resolutions the week following Christmas, and then hold a New Year's Resolution party on New Year's Day, and award gifts.

INVENTORY REDUCTION SALE

Start the New Year off with an inventory reduction sale, offering low prices so the store can beat the annual personal property taxes, which are based on January inventory. Stress that these savings will be passed on only to early-bird customers shopping January 1.

Valentine's Day

Retailers can spur sales by doing a bit of novel hearts-and-flowers promotion to entice customers. Try these:

HEARTS-AND-FLOWERS ROUTINE:

Use any type of hearts-and-flowers contest; using love letters or essays on why a certain girl or mom is the best is always good.

ST. VALENTINE

Build a promotion around St. Valentine; do some research on the historic figure and find out something about him on which to launch an event. Or hold a contest for the most unusual bit of information customers submit regarding the saint, about whom little is usually mentioned.

VALENTINE TREATS

Greet customers during Valentine promotional activity with a box of candy on the counter, inviting them to help themselves. Or give a token box of candy to those purchasing gifts at the store.

FREE CARDS

Give free Valentine cards to those buying gifts.

SWEETHEART CONTEST

Hold a Valentine contest with men writing why their sweethearts or wives should be named this year's Valentine. Can be done on group basis or by individual retailer. Consider a Valentine dance, complete with crowning of the Valentine queen, if on a group basis.

SWEETHEART SALE

Use higher priced merchandise, reduce it, and offer liberal credit terms, advertising it as a "sweetheart of a sale."

Washington's Birthday

Another popular holiday which gains in retail status each year.

BIRTHDAY PARTY

Dress clerks in costumes typical of Washington's Birthday. Bake 22 (or the number which corresponds to the date of the holiday for that year) capsules into a huge cake, with the one containing the number 15 the grand prize winner. Serve cherry ice cream and cherry pie with coffee.

CHERRY TREES AND HATCHETS

Both lend themselves well to promotional use. Real cherry trees can be given away—or sold at 22 cents each. So do flags and pictures of Washington.

REMEMBER MARTHA

Give it a new twist and include Martha. Build a promotion for the ladies centered around Martha.

WE "CANNOT TELL A LIE"

That's a great slogan and lends itself well to promotional activity.

PRICING

Use prices with the number 22; e.g., 22¢, $10.22; $22.

CHERRY-TREE PRIZES

Go back a few years and capture the flair of the old country-church fair. Use a cherry-tree gift idea. Roll wads of red paper, each with a number inside, and hang from a fake cherry tree. Under it have an assortment of gifts, each with a number on them. Either by contest or other device (give a chance with each purchase), let customers pick a cherry. They receive the gift under the tree whose number coincides with the number in the cherry they choose.

BEST-DRESSED

Stage a contest for the best-dressed customer most typical of

George or Martha. (You might use this for the sales staff to encourage enthusiasm and to lend atmosphere.)

CHERRY PIES

Ideal giveaways. Try a year's supply (one a week) as the grand prize in a contest. Gain publicity midway through the year by running a picture as the winner receives his 25th pie.

CAMP-OUT

Just as Washington and his army camped out in the middle of winter—so can the store and its customers. Give an award to anyone who spends the birthday night on the store parking lot. In one city a group of Boy Scouts arrived early with tents and spent the night. The publicity gained was tremendous.

PICTURE OF GEORGE

Use a "Picture of George" contest for group promotion. Fasten dollar bills on posters with the wording "Here's your picture of George." Pick names at random from the city directory (phone book) and post these in store windows—or in the store. Customers must visit stores to claim their picture of George, which is the bill.

To stimulate interest through the day, add new names every hour, or post an entirely new selection of names every hour.

Lincoln's Birthday

Copy ideas from "George" above which might be adaptable and from which promotions around Lincoln can be personalized.

Easter

Easter is the time for spring fashion shows—summer merchandise showings—parades.

Like Christmas, this is big buying time, and retail groups will do well to work together to promote not only Easter but spring

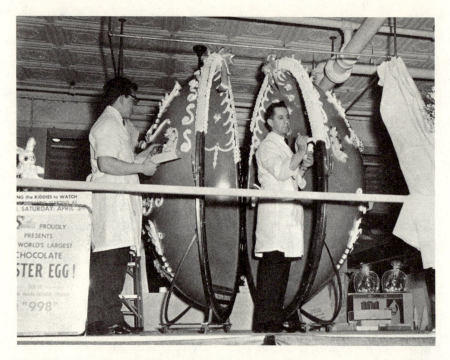

Sattler's Dept. Store, Buffalo, N.Y., feels this "World's Largest Chocolate Easter Egg" is their best promotional gimmick. The 700-pound egg is decorated on the main floor of the store for all customers to see. (Courtesy of Sattler's Dept. Store)

and summer. The entire season can be swept off in one gigantic promotion.

ANIMAL GIVEAWAYS

These have reportedly been good in the past. But they have received severe criticism too, and some of it apparently has been justified. Reports of mistreatment of baby chicks and bunnies are heard each Easter. Many humane groups recommend live animal giveaways be stopped.

Stores promoting around live animals should insure that each animal will have a good home and be well cared for by its owner.

SUBSTITUTE STUFFED ANIMALS

Huge stuffed animals pull as well, often even better than live animals. Try them as giveaways, thus eliminating parental objection, which often accompanies live-animal gifts.

SPRING FASHION SHOWS

This is the time to feature attire for the entire family. Zero in on all members instead of just mom and girls, as has been traditional.

Sprinkle fashion shows with a spring or Easter theme, refreshments, contests, token gifts. Use women or teen groups as models.

HAT CONTESTS

Work out a simple one with rules stipulating the items used to decorate the hat must be available in the average home—or purchased in the store.

Do it as an attraction at a fashion show. Supply basic hats, or have spectators bring them along. The store supplies pins, tape, string, and staples to be used in fastening trims, and a selection of materials (anything and everything) with which women style their hats. Give the ladies three to five minutes in which to make their creations.

Or have the women create their hats at home and wear them to the style show, with prizes awarded.

Another angle is to have the hats displayed in store windows, with a winner selected and a prize awarded.

Winners can have their picture taken in their Easter bonnets, to be used in advertising and publicity.

You might also stage a grand Easter parade in the store, with women modeling their entries and a winner chosen.

EGG HUNTS

These are ideal on a retail-group basis. Use a park, large yard, or wooded area. Or try the shopping district if it is mall-like and lends itself to such an activity.

Use colors to designate prize categories, with the gold egg the grand winner. Divide hunt area into sections for various age groups or give little folks a head start. Liven up the event by having Easter bunny appear, passing out jelly eggs from a giant basket.

Insist adults stay out of the hunt area—to make it truly a children's event.

EASTER PARADES

Retailers working with local groups can make this almost as popular as the traditional Christmas parade. Have church groups participate, if it is to be a family affair, with congregations marching under their church banners, and gifts given to the church with the largest turnout.

Or give it strictly a teen-agers' or children's approach.

JELLY-EGG CONTESTS

Display a basketful of jelly eggs and have customers guess how many there are.

PETS FOR THE ZOO

Emphasize that live pets won't be used as giveaways, but instead that a pet will be donated to the local zoo for all to enjoy.

A name-the-pet contest can be held to build enthusiasm, with the winner making the actual presentation to the zoo. Have the pet in the store for a day or two so customers can get acquainted.

STORE MASCOT

Pets make welcome additions to stores. One store used a monkey, which became the delight of child shoppers.

Similar store mascots can be used to entertain little folks. Even adults become fond of these and will stop to say hello. During the year, advertising and promotion can be geared around the mascot, with ads saying, "Polly says, '(advertising message)'."

EASTER FLOWER SHOW

Try this for something different, awarding prizes for the best entry. One classification can be limited to Easter theme entries. Include artificial and wildflower categories.

Spring Time

Shake off winter doldrums and brighten up the retail scene with hanging planters filled with flowers, window boxes and displays including color in bright splashes.

FLOWER SHOWS

Stage these, or flower competitions, using local florists for judges. Or hold floral-arrangement classes or demonstrations.

WHITE DOVES AND CHERRY BLOSSOMS

These lend themselves well to spring decor and themes for promotional efforts. This is an ideal time to stage a cherry-tree contest (See Washington's birthday.)

SEASONAL REFRESHMENTS

Dispense with hot coffee and switch to iced tea for refreshments.

MOVE OUTDOORS

Get the jump on summer outdoor sales by having an early-bird outdoor event in the spring.

DEMONSTRATIONS

Kick off the summer demonstration season with early events designed around outdoor cooking and living, complete with samples for spectators. Landscaping seminars and sports shows featuring recreational vehicles are good.

GARDENING

Highlight the green-thumb bit early. Demonstrations, classes, contests, and exhibits built around gardening will pull, with resource people available at county extension offices and from manufacturing firms.

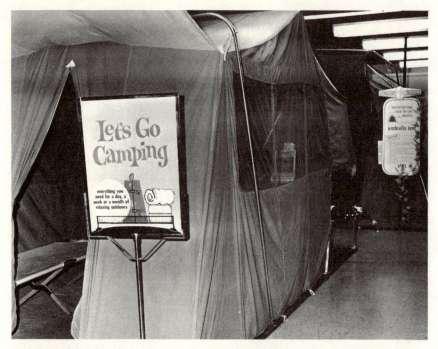

Sears, Chicago, displayed tents, completely equipped, to aid sales and also make customers aware of all the items necessary for outdoor living. (Courtesy of Fairchild Visuals)

ECOLOGY

This is the time to promote spring cleanups on a community basis. Include students, garden clubs, and conservation groups, and zero in on a dirty river bank, a filled ditch, roadside areas. Stores can furnish leadership, snacks, and prizes.

Mothers' and Fathers' Days

These two old standbys are a must; imaginative gimmicks include:

KING OR QUEEN FOR A DAY

Need more be said? Such contests held separately on the individual days, or jointly by promoting the days as a single event, lend themselves to retail efforts.

WINNERS' EVENING OUT

Winners in Mothers' and Fathers' Day contests can receive corsages, an evening at the theater, dinner for two; or make it a really grand gift with a night in a fine hotel and baby-sitting service provided at home.

OLDEST MOTHER—YOUNGEST MOTHER

Both are good for contest ideas. Or you might try to find the mother with the most children—or the most adopted children.

DON'T FORGET GRANDMA AND GRANDPA

Honor the oldest grandma or grandpa in the community. Perhaps a contest for the one—or the couple—with the most grandchildren.

FASHION SHOWS

These can be adapted to Mothers' Day events, inviting fathers as honored guests.

SPECIAL GIFT TABLES

This is the time when special gift-suggestion tables can be placed near the front of the store to make shopping easy for dads and small fry.

CHILDREN'S SHOPPING HOURS

Set aside special hours, perhaps on a Saturday morning, when young children can shop alone. Use low tables and special price ranges; have understanding and helpful clerks available; publish listings beforehand which mom can check and send along for suggestions; give a token gift to small shoppers.

MY MOM (OR DAD) IS TOPS

Take it from there. An ideal theme around which to build an essay contest. Work through schools, if preferred.

Children's Day

This holiday is often overlooked, but shouldn't be. Many families celebrate it, and more probably would if retailers would promote it.

Basically, use the same gimmicks to urge parents to honor their children as are used for Mothers' or Fathers' Day. Prizes can be given to the couple with the most children or the most grandchildren; or to the couple who has taken in the most adopted or foster children through the years.

The gimmick is to make the prizes something the children will enjoy.

Halloween

The spooky season can be thrilling and colorful as a retail event. Try these.

JACK-O-LANTERN

Try carving contests with pumpkins displayed in retail stores and windows. Prizes can go to the most unusual, largest, smallest, most highly decorated, spookiest, with the last the grand prize winner.

PUMPKIN SALES

Provide outdoor space for rural kids who have pumpkins to sell to display their produce. Just publicize the event—the kids will take it from there—with urban kids bartering and dickering with rural kids.

OLD WITCHES AND PUMPKIN MEN

These characters can wander through the store during Halloween promotions to stir interest and award prizes.

STORE-WINDOW DECORATING CONTEST

These are very popular with youth. Often school art classes

can be used to compete for prizes. Or retailers can assign windows to students on an individual basis.

WITCHIN' FRIDAY

Build an event around a bewitchin' Friday evening—letting the imagination work. Black cats, witches' brew, ghosts, wide-eyed owls, goblins, skeletons, and other Halloween figures can be worked into theme, decor, contests, and prizes.

FREE RIDES FOR TRICK-OR-TREATERS

Work to get little goblins off the streets early. Either alone or with community groups, retailers can sponsor a party for various age groups starting at 8 p.m. Make it free, asking city, school, and church recreational directors to help out; work out games and contests with a Halloween theme; award prizes and provide treats. Arrange transportation home for children who may not have rides, so they are kept off the streets. A goodwill event, this will also reduce "tricks" in both residential and retail districts.

Or let retailers provide treats for all the children, asking parents to restrict door-to-door trick-or-treating, because of recent adverse publicity about contaminated candies. This can be handled at a central location, complete with organized recreational activities. School, church, and other groups will be anxious to participate.

Leap Year

This is the time to honor that group often neglected throughout the year—single people.

STILL-SINGLE CONTESTS

Have single men register; if they are still single a year later, they receive gifts.

HOOKED HIM

Women register; those who get married during the year are honored with a wedding gift.

These gimmicks will build publicity later. Interest can be kept alive by printing lists in ads during the year of the women who have caught their men—and of the men who are still eligible for the big grand prize.

SINGLES PARTIES

Bring in consultants to demonstrate how to decorate a bachelor pad; hold demonstrations on cooking for one (or intimate parties for two), or on sporting activities and other things of interest to single people.

SINGLES CLUB

Form a singles club, for both men and women, working with civic and other groups to provide something for these people to do, with meetings whenever members decide to hold them.

LATE BLOOMERS GET CROWNED

Why not crown the oldest bachelor in the community? The oldest woman to get married during the year can be queen.

Or pick the two oldest who are still single and crown them both—imagine the publicity if a romance were to bloom later.

RECIPE SWAPS

A good mixer to get things rolling at a singles event. Add a category for the best recipe on "how to stay single."

PLAY CUPID

Advertise that the store wants to play Cupid. Sponsor a singles-get-together—either for everyone or for specific age groups: teen-agers, middle-agers, or golden-agers. Why not invite them all to come and do their thing?

St. Patrick's Day

With the many slogans, colors, and costumes that surround this day, no retailer should be at a loss for ideas. You might include:

Jordan Marsh, Boston, built a St. Patrick's Day display around a variety of products. Use your imagination! (Courtesy of Fairchild Visuals)

IRISH RECIPES

Irish cakes, coffees, breads—you name it. Contests, sales, and similar events can be staged around these, including Irish recipe swaps.

SHAMROCKS, GREEN, IRISH MUSIC

All lend themselves well to themes, decor, background, and contests.

ST. PADDY'S DAY DANCE

For adults or teens, or on a come-one-come-all basis.

IRISH POTLUCK

What a way to get acquainted! Set up tables, chairs, and benches, and tell residents to come on down and get acquainted. Stipulate only that each person must wear something green.

Make it a real potluck. No pre-planning. Each family brings something for the gigantic community buffet. Merchants can contribute dessert or a green punch for beverage.

If held on a group basis, hours can be from 6 to 7 p.m., with "Irish buys" available in the stores from 7 to 9 p.m.

Give prizes for those in the best Irish costume.

TRIP TO THE OLD SOD

An ideal grand prize for a St. Patrick's contest.

Thanksgiving and Fall

What a combination!

With Thanksgiving as a grand finale, and just before the Holidays, build fall promotions early and let the Thanksgiving weekend wrap them up and open the door to the next.

HARVEST TIME

This lends itself well to sales, costumes, gimmicks, and contests.

HELPING LOCAL CHARITIES

Two more ideas around which to build community-oriented promotions. Give a percentage of the day's sale to a local charity as a way of saying, "Thanks".

LOCAL CROPS AND PRODUCTS

All are good for displays, contests, and demonstrations during harvest days. Use these items in store windows. Hold contests for children growing the largest pumpkin or sunflower.

MISS ''FALL FESTIVAL''

Select a Fall Harvest Queen, and use her throughout the year to promote area products and industry.

HARVEST HOEDOWN

A great idea for something different but with the flavor of fall. Square dances, old-time prices, box lunches, and other old-fashioned ideas can be used.

COUNTRY FAIR

Turn the shopping-center area into an old-fashioned country fair. Let everyone bring homemade items for display or selling in outdoor booths. Give prizes for the best entries in baking, sewing, crocheting, arts and crafts, gardening, and floral competitions.

Have schools join in with spelling bees.

Hayrides, square dancing, and corn husking will add color.

HONOR AREA FARMERS

If yours is a rural area, sponsor an urban-rural get-together and name the Farmer of the Year. Extension office officials can help here.

HONOR INDUSTRIAL WORKERS

Get to know area industrial workers. These are the best potential customers in the community, because they receive pay checks regularly. Stage industrial coffee breaks, with retail-group representatives taking coffee and donuts to each shift in each local plant, spending the coffee-break period getting to know the workers. Most officials will cooperate.

HONOR RETAIL EMPLOYEES

Use this period to honor the people involved in retailing. After hours throw a gala affair for employees and their spouses; or hold a fall picnic for all retail employees and their families. Have old-fashioned games, prizes, refreshments.

HISTORICAL THANKSGIVING

Rely on history for costumes, promotional ideas, and themes. Pilgrims and Indians are colorful. Display early historic items; give away antiques or reproductions as prizes in retail promotions.

FALL WINDOW-DISPLAY EXHIBITS

These can include old items lent by residents which relate to harvest time or the community history.

ANTIQUE SHOWS

Stress the colonial angle with antique shows or exhibits. Demonstrations of antique items can be worked into fall promotional ventures.

COMMUNITY HERITAGE

This is the time to promote the community's heritage. Emphasize its history in a fall promotion, using a vacant building as a center for exhibits and displays.

THANKSGIVING FASHION SHOW

Kick off the upcoming Christmas season with a Thanksgiving fashion show or gift show. Turkey sandwiches, corn muffins, pumpkin tarts can be served, with a Christmas turkey as a giveaway prize.

THANKSGIVING SCHOOL CONTESTS

This is the time to work with history and English teachers for school-oriented contests. Results can be displayed in store windows.

LAST OUTDOOR EVENT OF THE SEASON

Wrap up summer outdoor selling programs with a gala fall outdoor sale or festival. Art and cultural shows can be included, with area groups participating. Churches, which normally hold bazaars, can be included, setting up booths during the event. Or try a fall flea market.

DEMONSTRATIONS

Turkey-carving demos are good at this time. Christmas cooking and decorating demonstrations and Christmas workshops can be held early.

Hunters

Don't forget this category, as these people can increase volume tremendously if they can be lured in. Ideas include:

HUNTER REGISTRATIONS

Out-of-town hunters register their names and temporary addresses. Postal cards are available to be mailed (by the store) to their families back home. Hunters don't generally write letters, so families will appreciate this. In event of emergency, the family knows where to contact the hunter, as the store name is stamped on the card, with the notation that the store has registered the hunter. If emergencies arise, store immediately contacts local officials.

Hunters can notify the store each day if they are going out of the area.

Stores can work with area citizen-band radio enthusiasts to assist in emergencies, by using walkie-talkie and radio hams in helping police search areas.

DEER AND GAME DISPLAYS

Provide a central deer pole or game display area where game can be hung. Free coffee and sandwiches for hunters as they gather each evening will be appreciated; stage contests for the largest game hung each day.

HUNTERS' FEAST

Sponsor a hunters' feast at the end of the season, or midway through. Hunters who have been successful contribute—or have one or two retailers provide the meat. Area conservation clubs and men's groups will help.

Or have local sportsmen contribute game (pheasant, woodcock, coon, rabbit, etc) during the year. This can be kept frozen until the deer season (the big hunting event in most areas) rolls around. Then a community game feast can be held. Stores can tie in with a hunter-promotion the same evening.

HUNTING CHECKLIST

Hunters always forget something. Locate tables near the front of the store, stocking items which hunters most frequently need. Provide camp-supply lists (often available from conservation departments) on what is needed to stock a hunting camp.

IMPULSE BUYING

Make the most of in-store traffic when hunting gear is being purchased. Make this shopping easy by staging one or two evening events when gifts in a wide price range will be available.

Keep these informal—most of the hunters will shop in their outdoor hunting attire and will be uncomfortable if the atmosphere is formal.

AREA INFORMATION

This is a must for an influx of out-of-town hunters. Have maps of the area available; be able to direct and guide hunters to various locations. Open up—pass along good hunting spots. Satisfied hunters return; dissatisfied hunters do not.

PROVIDE FREE PICTURES

Offer to take free pictures of successful hunters, to be sent to the hunters' home-town papers, along with details of each kill. The publicity gained in enticing future hunters will be worth the cost involved.

(See chapter 21 on tourism for ideas on how to promote the area and attract tourists.)

9

Downtown Strategy: Unite or Perish

The 1960s spotlighted the plight of the downtown area. So much adverse publicity was received that many believe the central business district (CBD) is already dead. Unfortunately, retailers sometimes helped create the devastating image by chronic complaining. The picture painted was one of woe; if shoppers hadn't already given up the CBD, many more did after hearing merchant complaints about what was wrong and why the town was dying.

Regardless of past history, the CBD is a vital part of the retail scene. Dying downtowns can be rejuvenated. In the fight for survival the CBD must be equipped to compete with shopping centers, which continue to grow and spread. Roads are built at ever increasing rates and the mobile age quickens. No longer are customers homebound. Unless CBD retailers meet their competition, customers will travel outside the community on shopping trips.

Community loyalty is no longer freely given; customers demand many things in return. Traditional ties are being broken. New people move in—lifelong residents move out.

The CBD and its rebirth may well be one of the most vital elements in the years ahead if retailers in the downtown rise and accept the challenge. Progressive retailers can band together and start a revitalization project rolling—encouraging others to join in.

COMMUNITY UNITY

This is an ideal method of stimulating action, but it is often hard. Though 100 percent participation is desirable, don't hesitate to hold group events if a few merchants refuse to participate. Customers DO pay attention to sponsors of community-wide projects, and before long holdouts will seek to be included.

Community programs offer a real challenge and are rewarding in many ways. They may be used to obtain volume fast; to keep people shopping locally; as a demonstration of community spirit with no direct selling involved; to combat consumer criticism of "cold unfriendliness;" and to spruce up the retail district. They engender goodwill and community spirit by emphasizing cultural and civic themes.

If physical revitalization of the downtown is needed, the job may not always be inexpensive or easy. Investments may be needed, with re-building required; new fronts or even entire new stores may be necessary; vacant shops must be filled; new advertising and promotional efforts must be directed toward a new image.

Professional promoters may be needed.

But the first step is to get organized.

Gimmicks to Start United CBD Efforts

ORGANIZE AND PLAN

Concerned retailers can meet, formulate basic plans, and present these at a general meeting later. If enthusiasm can be built, even if not among all, begin carrying out the program. Plans should be sound enough and permanent enough to meet CBD needs, but flexible enough to permit changes to satisfy all.

In organizational and planning meetings, determine to bury old feuds and forget about what might have been. New organizers must hold a tight rein on meetings, refusing to let discussion become bogged down in personal vendettas and personality clashes.

If pledges are to be a part of the project, start collection immediately, weeding out those who pledge but don't pay.

TAKE A TOUR—AND OBSERVE

It may be necessary to convince some that something must be done. Do this by taking a tour: gathering retailers together and visiting outlying shopping centers and other metropolitan shopping districts. Sight in on how they provide gigantic, well-lighted parking lots; watch how they promote together, how they provide attractive shopping and rest facilities, how they use a variety of shops for greater drawing power. Note that, while each store in a shopping center has its own personality, they are all part of a unified group, projecting a solid community image.

Note especially how competition looms in shopping centers . . . there is no maintaining of status quo, no keeping competition out. Much of the success of these centers is based on the numerous shops, which attract because customers know if they don't find exactly what they want in one store, they may in another.

TOUR YOUR OWN COMMUNITY, TOO

Take a "constructive-criticism" tour of your own shopping district. Note liabilities and seek spontaneous suggestions on how these can be corrected. Try to see the shopping dictrict through the eyes of the customer.

ASK LOCAL SHOPPERS WHAT THEY WANT

Take a survey (often a nearby college will have a retailing department which will conduct this). Find out what shoppers want; what they dislike about their local CBD; where they shop and why.

Such a survey will also reveal primary and secondary shopping areas and detail which areas are being lost to the competition. Retailers can then work harder to entice people back.

Building a New Image for the CBD

Much can be involved here, with the scope ranging from reshaping a worn-out CBD physically to gaining a new attitude about it in the minds of area residents. Only retailers in the individual CBDs can determine what is needed.

Here are some suggestions and gimmicks:

SERVE CUSTOMERS

Resolve that retailers have a responsibility to serve customers and gear efforts toward pleasing them. Unfortunately, many in the

CBD have taken customers for granted, forgetting that service and courtesy are also important.

SET AN EXAMPLE—SHOP AT HOME

Gone are the days when it was sophisticated for the business-man's family to take extended shopping trips to large metropolitan areas. Times have changed. The mobile age is here, and everyone can now go out of town to shop.

Retailers who expect loyalty from their community can set the example by shopping at home themselves.

HELP FAILING BUSINESSES

Retailers often have the power to help a failing or floundering business or facility within the core area. As an example, recent years have seen the decline of theaters and hotels in the CBD. Both were once, and still can be, major attractions. Spot those businesses in decline before they sprout "closed" signs, and work toward helping them stay in business. If necessary, gear retail promotions around them, offering their services as prizes in retail efforts; e.g., free tickets to the movies, dinner at the hotel.

ELIMINATE THE NEON JUNGLE, CONGESTION AND CONFUSION

Clutter and confusion often reign in older retail districts, as each merchant endeavors to outdo his neighbor in the rush for bright lights and color. The result is a gaudy, confusing effect which detracts from rather than complements the scene. With a united effort, situations like this can be eliminated and a co-ordinated effect attained.

Eliminate congestion and confusion by removing outdated posters, unnecessary signs. Overhead wires can go underground. Many eyesores can be removed, with a pleasant, serene atmosphere emerging.

UNITED ARCHITECTURAL THEME

Pick a theme to which all store fronts, interiors, and other physical aspects of the CBD can be geared. Typical is the Tyrolean or Swiss look to which many resort areas have turned. A new look, especially when many stores are involved, is an attraction in itself.

Projects like this can be contagious. Procrastinators often join in later. Community events can be spearheaded with the new image.

PARKING PLACES

A must in the CBD and when the downtown is being rejuvenated, they should be included in plans. (See the next chapter on RX for Parking Ills for specific ideas.)

SCULPTURE, FOUNTAINS, REFLECTING POOLS, PLANTERS

All of these, plus music, shrubs, flowers, shade trees, park benches, newsstands, trash containers, good lighting, courtesy telephones, rest areas are among items a CBD can provide, often inexpensively, to compete with shopping centers.

PROMOTIONAL DEPARTMENTS

Just as shopping centers have found these important, so will CBDs. A promotional office, with staff adequate to handle group needs, is almost a must if joint activity is to be successful. The office can also double as an information center for the CBD.

RESTORE HISTORIC FACILITIES IN THE RETAIL AREA

Typical of what a united group of retailers and businessmen can do, along with community support, is the restoration of the Chicago Auditorium. President Benjamin Harrison headed a delegation at its dedication in 1889; Caruso sang there, as did other stars; but by the 1940s it had closed its doors. It reopened in 1967 after a seven-year drive with 9,000 individuals, corporations, foundations, and other groups contributing.

Although a renovation of this size isn't needed in most communities, almost every CBD has a similar historic site which can be reclaimed as a vital element. What better project for the retail group than restoration of a bit of its history?

SALUTE LONG-TIME RETAILERS

Boost the retail image by saluting those who have managed to stay in business for a long period of time. Instead of the store's going it alone with an anniversary promotion, the entire retail community can join in for a grand celebration.

COVER FRINGE AREAS

Consider fringe areas of the CBD in planning, and include these streets as an integral part of the overall plans. Fringe areas serve well for apartment complexes for the elderly; for young working couples who may prefer to live close to the CBD; for single persons; for those who do not have cars. Such fringe-area living facilities will reduce parking problems, cut congestion, and put a number of customers on the immediate outskirts of the CBD.

Frequently older homes, also going into disrepair, are located in these areas. Retail-oriented restoration can lead toward developing these into women's club headquarters, apartment complexes, or old-fashioned tourist homes, which are needed but often not available in many communities.

OPEN-AIR MARKET

In a rural area, provide a farmers' market where booths can be rented and fresh produce sold.

REDUCE NOISE, HUSTLE, BUSTLE

Normally associated with the CBD, these are frequently cited as the reason some persons don't like to shop downtown.

Reduce these offenses, if they cannot be eliminated. Seek to have horn blowing restricted and try to get police enforcement of similar noise nuisance laws; re-route truck traffic, if possible; remove fire stations and police headquarters to fringe areas; re-route highway traffic off the main street, if possible.

OLD STREET LIGHTING FIXTURES

Renovate old lighting. Women especially like well-lighted streets, shopping areas, and parking lots. Frequently arrangements can be made with municipal or utility officials to finance these improvements over a period of years.

DOWNTOWN HOTEL

This is a facility which can be the headquarters for community and visitor programs. Unfortunately, in many CBDs the downtown hotels have fallen into disrepute; many have closed and stand as boarded up monuments to a dead era. Bring them back to life. Many groups have been successful in restoring their downtown hotels, retaining the fine old architecture and using it to promote the community's heritage.

Some retail groups, unsuccessful in finding new private owners, have formed corporations and opened hotels as joint efforts.

Not only will clients doing business in the CBD prefer to stay there, but shoppers can be enticed downtown by hotel-oriented promotions. A good hotel can make the CBD come alive; provide needed meeting rooms; entice conventions and other outside groups. (See chapter 21 on tourism for convention ideas.)

BLOCK-BY-BLOCK BASIS

If it is impossible for the entire CBD to be renovated at once, try a block-by-block method, working out details among retailers involved. Publicize what is going on, and hold block parties as each section is completed.

MINOR FACE-LIFTING

If a complete remodeling job isn't warranted, try a minor face-lifting, with painting and sandblasting where needed.

SECOND STORIES CAN BE ATTRACTIVE

Customers see more than the ground level. There is nothing more hideous than a job partially done. Regardless of how nice the ground floor fronts look, customers will notice the untouched second and third stories.

Often left to ruin, unpainted, dirty, and with broken or boarded-up windows, these upper stories detract from and contrast sharply with renovated ground levels. With little effort and investment, the upper floors can be cleaned on the outside, even if nothing is done on the inside. (Don't overlook the second floor as storage area.)

One gimmick is to paint all upper level fronts the same color. This permits stores to maintain individual images at the ground level, but provides low-cost overall harmony and balance to the rest of the CBD.

DOWNTOWN MOVIE THEATER

As well as their hotels, many downtowns have lost their theaters. Stage a comeback. Reopen theaters and turn them into community facilities. Frequently all that is needed is a minor investment in improved screens, sound equipment, and a good cleaning job. Form a retail corporation to reopen the theater if private enterprise can't be found to do it.

Couple the downtown theater and its comeback with retail promotional efforts (free tickets as prizes) to bring it back to life. Have the theater serve the CBD with free Saturday afternoon kiddie matinees, fashion shows, art and cultural fairs, demonstrations, workshops; permit area clubs to use it at a small fee or on a percentage basis, bringing civic and cultural presentations to the community again.

Sponsor theater parties and hold local talent shows to keep interest.

RETURN TO THE OUTDOORS

Sell outdoors throughout the summer by placing tables and racks in doorway areas to entice customers to stop and look. Tables, chairs, planters, lanterns, and snack counters can be easily set up and taken down.

Urge restaurants to open sidewalk cafés, even if only occasionally.

Or go all out and provide an outdoor background and theme by installing gas lights, canopies, courts with an old-time or European sidewalk personality.

LOUNGE AREAS

Another must. Every CBD should have some lounge areas, well marked.

SICK CENTER OR FIRST-AID STATION

Just a small service, but greatly appreciated for emergencies, which do arise. A simple first-aid service provided in the CBD informational or promotional center may suffice.

RECREATIONAL FACILITIES

Miniature game areas including things like shuffleboard courts, golf, or table tennis can be provided. Tables for card playing, or even an outdoor TV area for those who are waiting, will provide a much-appreciated service.

BRIDGED WALKWAYS

If the CBD is old, with multi-level buildings, consider bridging some of the stores at the second or third levels, so people can cross the street without going outside.

Benefits are numerous: customers can go across the street

A novel attraction, like this huge slide, can draw crowds and provide activity in the central business district. Charge a small fee for the rides and the promotion will pay its own way.

without going outside; crossways can be attractive and draw curious customers to the area; the bridged walkways can serve as snack shops, lounge areas, or cultural exhibit areas.

CHILDREN'S ACTIVITIES

These are a must: young parents now expect them. Free movies are good, but consider providing roped-off areas with safe toys where children can play. During peak promotional periods, when stores are crowded, supervision may be necessary.

DO AWAY WITH CURBS

Slant sidewalks to slope gently to the street level. This makes walking easier; makes pushing baby buggies and strollers a cinch; and is an asset to the handicapped, as well as the elderly. Sidewalks and streets are easier to clean.

FILL VACANT BUILDINGS

This can be a major project and is often best handled by a special committee concentrating on finding new businesses. Start with owners: obtain permission to keep windows cleaned and filled with community-type displays to eliminate the vacant look. Learn square footage, facilities available in the building, and rental or selling price so efforts can be made to find buyer or tenant.

(Schools and area groups will provide materials for window use.)

SECOND HOMES

Renovate dilapidated upper stories in the CBD, or immediate fringe area, and provide inexpensive small apartment units. Business-men and others working in the CBD may find it convenient to keep a small apartment or room.

Groups may turn them into headquarters; individuals giving dancing or music lessons will quickly become tenants if rent is attractive.

ARCHITECTURAL INNOVATION

Consult with engineers and architects (often available in the area) for novel ideas to make the CBD outstanding. Typical would be a moving sidewalk, gigantic, odd-shaped, permanent umbrellas in rest areas, huge slides for children and adults, unusual fountains or sculptures.

One different, truly unique item alone can stimulate much interest and traffic.

REAR ENTRANCES

Another item frequently let go. Don't forget to clean up rear alleys. Make rear entrances out of them. Remove unused fire escapes, which often hang grotesquely from buildings; replace overflowing rubbish cans with hinged refuse receptacles.

With sidewalks, removal of clutter, a fresh paint job, some blacktop, and a few planters, a pleasant rear-entranceway can be achieved.

If adjoining retailers co-operate, a dreary alley can be turned into a small parking lot—ideal for employees.

EXECUTIVE PARKS

Executives and professionals like to locate in CBDs . . . if the area is alive. Often these people have much in common, so group their offices together to form an executive park. These people are an asset, for one thing, because they generate traffic.

CIVIC CENTERS, LIBRARIES, CULTURAL CENTERS

These are also good in CBD developments. All draw traffic and provide services. Include them in plans when possible.

PEDESTRIAN CROSSWALKS

If traffic is a problem, build one of these over-the-street crosswalks in the CBD. It can be an attraction in itself.

CULTURAL EVENTS

Arrange—even sponsor—events like concerts, lectures, slide presentations, theater parties, operas, local events like rodeos, sheepshearing competitions, Indian ceremonial dances. Evening café dining, strolling singers, and strolling bands all generate activity. A teen center in the CBD can bring young customers in and give them a meeting place, taking them out of stores for their visiting, but having them nearby for the mass purchasing they do.

RESTORE DOWNTOWN CHARACTER

Cities are losing their character, critics say. They have too often become a mishmash of building and activity, devoid of atmosphere. Many have been renovated to the point where all heritage has been lost.

Restore CBD character by emphasing heritage and focusing on items remaining in the CBD which can be used to provide character, history, a touch of nostalgia.

GATHERING PLACE

Downtowns came into being as the community gathering place.

With its traditional and expansive area, the CBD can regain this image and attract people again. All they need is a reason to return. Don't leave any idea uncovered in trying to bring people in—not only for retail purposes (this will be an automatic side benefit), but for visiting, community, professional, cultural, religious, and other events.

Park areas, municipal-building lawns (which all too frequently have grown "keep off the grass" signs in recent years), malls, benches in front of stores, and similar devices can be used to make the CBD a place in which to congregate.

SERVICE FACILITIES

Customers will bring cars for repairs, laundry to be washed and cleaned, shoes to be fixed into the CBD if such services are available. Service facilities are a great retail asset and should be included, encouraged, and planned for.

ONE-STOP BILI PAYING

A central location in the CBD for bill paying is another gimmick to entice people to shop there. Utility, phone, and other bills can be easily paid while on shopping trips if a central location or service is provided. Sometimes arrangements can be made to have one retailer handle these.

Promotional Gimmicks

The preceding paragraphs deal primarily with physical gimmicks to rejuvenate the CBD. The following are ideas which can be used to build community goodwill, attract attention to the CBD, bring customers in, and provide novel touches to sales and other events.

ENCOURAGE DOWNTOWN LUNCHING

Encourage people working in the CBD to eat there. Employers can join together to stagger lunch hours. With the traditional noon-to-1 p.m. lunch hour, restaurants are often crowded, waiting is necessary, service is poor, and diners rushed. There is little time left for shopping. Yet the lunch-hour employee trade can be lucrative if there is time to eat and shop too.

Let employees (who may want to lunch and shop together—or who have family obligations) choose the lunch hours they desire. Restaurants and their help will benefit by spreading the work load over two hours.

EMPLOYMENT BUREAU

A Chamber of Commerce or retail group can operate an informal employment bureau or booth, providing a vital service for residents. Retailers seeking full or part-time help are served, as are professional firms in the area. A simple recipe-card index file will permit persons job hunting to list name, address, and type of job in which they are interested. No other details are needed—they can be obtained by prospective employers later during interviews. Firms needing help check the cards and make their own contacts.

Include high-school and college youths, informing them of the service through school administrators. Mention the service in group ads.

RETAIL REBELLION

Everyone is rebelling nowadays. Why not the retailer?

Advertise a retail rebellion, with merchants taking a day off to elect group officers and conduct annual CBD business. This will provide needed time for the group; clerks can stage a great "boss is away" sale.

PROVIDE LOCKERS

Take a tip from metropolitan department stores which provide lockers for garments and purchases. If individual stores can do it, a small community can do this as a group, operating lockers from a central location, where people can store packages while shopping. No help is needed—lockers have their own keys.

DRINKING FOUNTAINS

Inexpensive, but appreciated. Don't forget the tots. Install some at ground level for them.

Or build elaborate ones of fieldstone with a natural spring atmosphere. Include perhaps a park effect around them, with benches, ashtrays, and carpeted area for children to rest.

COFFEE, SANDWICH, AND SOUP MACHINES

These are little extras but always appreciated. Vendor type, they require little service.

WINDOW DISPLAYS

Windows can be a store's best advertising, but they must be kept clean, interesting, and frequently changed.

Add character and diversity by inviting women's or youth groups (school retailing classes, home-furnishing classes, church and civic groups) to put in window displays. Have merchandise available to be displayed and let members come up with their own props. Give each group a gift.

When working with groups, emphasize that homemade signs detract if not attractively done. Include credits in the windows, listing the club which installed each display.

You might change the open effect of the window by sectioning it off into small areas which can be individually dressed.

Work contests around the best decorated windows. Let customers in on the action, voting for the window they feel was best dressed.

DOWNTOWN GLEE CLUB

Get musically oriented downtowners together and let them entertain in the CBD during promotions. Sponsor informal sing-alongs on specific nights; use youth groups to carol in the CBD.

ALERT SYSTEM

Avoid losses by keeping alert to bad-check passers, known shoplifters, and other emergency situations. (Profits retained can be as important as profits gained.) Arrange a system among stores for telephone message sending, known as a "telephone tree." Divide into blocks, with one person in each block to receive a call from the CBD promotional or information center, or local police department. From there on the telephone tree is worked and the word quickly spread.

This method can also be used for notifying members of emergency retail meetings.

CARTOON CHARACTER

Give the CBD its own image by designing a character to be used in posters, advertisements, and promotional events. Have the little fellow appear on parking-lot signs, shopping bags. The figure will quickly be identified with the CBD and will be a good image builder.

BRAND-NAME SALE

With the multitude of stores in the CBD, brand names can be emphasized. Hold a gigantic brand-name sale, with each store emphasizing specific brand-name items. Use price reductions, demonstrations, and contests.

Emphasis on the number of brand names available in the CBD can be made periodically by using ads alphabetically listing brand names available and the stores which sell them.

SUBURBAN DAYS

Draw customers from outlying suburban areas by zeroing in on specific areas on specific days and catering to customers from that area. Welcome posters in store windows can be used.

Honor residents of every suburb at some time, so none feel left out.

If necessary, run shuttle buses to the areas.

POLITICAL INVOLVEMENT

This is the age of involvement; and retailers can correct one of the bad images they have gained by getting into the political arena. Often retailers have shied away from controversy, feeling they might lose customers.

The opposite might very well be true. A lethargic fence-straddling position can do more harm than good. Many people respect those who take a position; customers are no exception.

Change the image—not necessarily by taking sides politically on controversial issues (although it probably won't hurt as much as some may think), but by sending a candidate from the community to each national or state political convention. Local party groups can select their representatives, with the retail group picking up the tab.

With both parties pressed for funds, financial assistance will be appreciated. Hold a promotion with some profits going into the political coffers, dividing them among parties represented in the community.

Help get teenagers involved by sending a teen representative (chosen by the local party) to each convention.

DISC JOCKEYS

These are popular fellows who have large followings. Use them, especially for teenage and young-married promotions.

Record hops are still good. Or originate promotional efforts around a disc-jockey program. Have the radio locate its mobile unit in the downtown area and actually broadcast from the CBD. This will draw travelers who will hear it on their car radios; it will also bring in stay-at-homes who are listening.

Let informality reign, have the disc jockey chat with shoppers as they pass his unit.

RADIO OR TV CHATTER PROGRAMS

Use a local station and sponsor weekly chatter programs, rotating retailers and employees to discuss a wide range of items, from politics to local problems. Give employees a chance to express their views, even if they differ from yours. Invite customers to get into the act.

The CBD will build an image of awareness of vital issues and of bringing them to the people. Do not shy away from current topics—but have the announcer stress that the program is a community service designed to promote discussion and bring forth ideas and solutions to problems. Most listeners will understand and appreciate the opportunity to be enlightened. A few will threaten to shop elsewhere because they heard something they didn't like, but this type is seldom satisfied, and they are often "here today-gone tomorrow-back next week" types—dissatisfied everywhere.

PROMOTIONS FOR NON-RETAILERS

A frequent criticism heard by non-retail members of the CBD is that everything is retail oriented, that all the group money is spent on retail promotions.

Reverse this. Gear some promotional efforts towards realtors, banks, insurance men, professional, cultural, service, educational, and other interests represented in the CBD. Work with them on promotions which will benefit their groups, knowing this will also provide traffic for stores. The events make non-retail firms feel they are more than just dues-paying members, and they will be more willing to participate in retail sales promotions when they are held.

NIGHT LIGHTING

Just because stores close at 9 p.m. doesn't mean the CBD has to fold up. Many residents long to take a late evening stroll after doors close.

Brighten up the CBD; advertise that lights will be on at night —at least to brighten windows. Urge residents to window shop, to take evening strolls; promote walking through the downtown area by providing benches or even midnight coffee now and then, especially when good movies or other activities will draw traffic during the evening.

Build promotions around window shopping, using a talk radio show to give prizes to telephone callers who know what item was spotlighted in store windows the night before.

LATCH ONTO A SLOGAN OR SONG

Catchy tunes and slogans are "in". A CBD can have its own. If retailers can't handle this, hire a professional firm to write one. Or hold a contest and let local people with a creative urge write one.

WELCOME BANNERS AND FLAGS

While the neon jungle is distracting, well placed "welcome" banners and flags have an organized look. These are good during specific events—also at convention time.

One northern Michigan community, which normally pulls traffic from Canada, put up Canadian, Michigan, and United States flags on the highway leading into the city. Retailers displayed them in front of their firms. In the downtown area, oval signs bearing the name of each state, along with small state flags, were on each light post. The community used the nicknames "City of the States" and "Avenue of Flags." Out-of-towners frequently wrote the Chamber of Commerce about how welcome they felt when visiting the community.

HOUSEKEEPING EXTENDS PAST THE FRONT DOOR

A very revolting sight is to see a CBD retailer sweeping the litter from his sidewalk onto the street just before he opens shop. Poor public relations—yes. Also costly, as tax dollars will be needed to clean up behind him, when with little effort debris swept from the sidewalk could have been disposed of inside.

Retail promotions highlighting community and CBD clean-ups are good. Businessmen can arrive early and scrub the downtown. Or hire local youths to do it.

CLERKS SHOULD BE INFORMED ABOUT DOWNTOWN

Frequently residents complain they can't find things in their neighborhoods. Often clerks in the CBD aren't familiar with adjoining stores and what they stock. They do not refer customers to nearby shops which could serve them.

Change this by promoting employee tours of the CBD during slack periods. Run CBD inventory ads, highlighting the many things available in the CBD. List items alphabetically, or by store inventory. Emphasis should be put on the multitude of items stocked. Provide alphabetical lists for clerk referral of items and the stores which stock them.

An "inventory" sale event could be tied in. Or hold a contest and have customers guess how many items are available.

List, periodically, in ads the many types of stores, professions, and services available.

PR FOR DOWNTOWN

Frequently CBDs have no public-relations program with the news media except for advertising purposes. Many newsworthy happenings in the business district go unrecorded, although they would have made interesting news stories or picture features.

Develop a PR program at the retail-group level. The PR staff or committee can meet regularly with retail-group members to learn what should be publicized and to discuss what has been going on. Later meetings with reporters (include all media serving the area) will get the word out.

Be truly effective and have the PR committee schedule regular meetings with reporters to discuss things in the CBD other than strictly retail sales and ads. DO NOT ATTEMPT TO USE THE PR AS A METHOD TO GAIN FREE ADVERTISING OF RETAIL SALES. NEWS REPORTERS WILL SPOT THIS QUICKLY AND FEEL THEY ARE BEING USED.

BRING 'EM BACK WITH COUPON BOOKS

Sell booklets containing coupons for frequently used items and services available in the CBD. Restaurants can include dinner tickets; apparel shops items of clothing; a beauty shop could offer a shampoo or set; etc. Total value of all the items is added up; a generous discount taken off; and the booklets sold to customers at the discounted price. (They can also be given as prizes during promotions.)

This will entice customers into patronizing local firms and will make this a habit as they continue to use the coupons.

Cost of printing is shared by participants.

Make coupons redeemable over a three- or six-month period; or sell less expensive booklets for shorter periods.

DOWNTOWN CLOWNS

Retailers and employees with a sense of humor and a flair for the dramatic should dress up as CBD clowns, entertaining at intervals during promotions, staging impromptu appearances during the year, and making themselves available to local clubs and organizations for guest appearances as well as playing unscheduled performances at orphanages, hospitals, homes for the elderly, and nursery schools.

This can result in good publicity and spur interest in promotional efforts.

WELCOME THE MILITARY

The people living in military installations should be treated as members of another suburb area. Invite them to shop the CBD; have special days and events for them; run shuttle buses to the base; include them in community activities.

During armed forces celebrations, throw a military ball, inviting the public so all can get acquainted.

Break the college-military barrier by getting the two groups together, if both are represented in the community. Have representatives of student groups participate in CBD military affairs.

Get really bold—stage talks between the two on radio chatter programs (outlined earlier in this chapter).

Honor a military man and his family each month, playing host for the weekend to the couple.

Arrange with military officials for retailer tours of the base and provide a retailer with whom the servicemen can go to church. This can be done by listing religious preferences of retailers co-operating. A serviceman wanting to go to church with a family merely calls a retailer and makes arrangements. (If the retailer is to be out of town for the weekend, he should arrange with someone else to be the host—don't let the serviceman feel he is imposing.)

ELECTION GIMMICKS

Assist both parties by sponsoring "call the voter" drives. Put wives to work on this PR project or provide phones for party members to use. Give it a novel twist by inviting members of both parties to phone from a central calling point in the CBD.

Provide cars to take voters to the polls; even baby-sitters.

Set up booths in the CBD before election day and ask each party to staff them, distributing literature, buttons, and brochures, and to have their candidates on hand to meet the public.

Take popularity polls with customers balloting and post daily counts to build interest.

Hold contests staged around how many voters will cast their ballot on election day.

Use ads to provide information on registration, precinct locations, and hours polls will be open.

MERCHANDISE FORUMS

Participating retailers provide instruction and demonstrations; e.g., furniture stores can stress decorating, bakeries can do cake decorating; apparel shops can teach how to select clothing. If the CBD is diversified enough, these can be scheduled on a regular basis, with different retailers participating.

Manufacturers, suppliers, local schools and universities can be used as resources along with retailers.

NO-SELLING TOURS

Close stores one night and invite customers on a CBD tour. Each store furnishes its own guides and hostesses, serves refreshments, offers gifts, stages promotions, and holds showings. Spectators browse around, or take guided tours, with no sales made.

The gimmick is to get the customer acquainted with the many items and services the store offers.

SPECIAL HOURS FOR THE WORKING GAL

Cater to the working gal after normal hours. These women can't take in the regular 9 to 5 activities, so stage repeat performances for them occasionally. Try a late-afternoon tea; an extended lunch hour on a slow day. Early-morning breakfasts are also good: open stores early for female workers during good promotional sales so they can participate; let management personnel play clerk during these early-morning events. Or start a Business Belles Club with catered luncheons once monthly, where the gals can meet retailers personally in a social climate.

Have a central suggestion box available for employee suggestions, gripes and desires.

Honor working gals by saluting one each month and giving a gift.

Give awards to employers opening their doors to the most women.

Word-of-mouth advertising by enthusiastic girls working in the CBD can be tremendous.

EQUAL TREATMENT FOR MEN

Reverse the gimmick and do the same for men. At special seasons, hunting, fishing, golf, etc., hold events at special hours for male workers who are busy from 9 to 5. Serve he-man snacks and have the coffee pot on. Let the gals run the store (bring in management wives if necessary).

Or let women employees take over while men employees take off for an afternoon of golf with the boss. Publicize the event and invite women to shop downtown during the "all-girl" promotional effort.

COMMUNITY CULTURE

Gain goodwill and promote cultural programs by underwriting a specific performance of a community group staging a play, concert, or lecture. Offer free tickets in a promotion.

Arrange with local theaters for theater parties to performances not on the regular schedule. Keep shops open after the performance and offer "After Matinee Specials."

PUT THE WELCOME MAT OUT FOR NEWCOMERS

If no professional franchised "welcome" service is operating in the community, farm the job out to a women's club or hire a local woman to handle it. Or turn the job over to a high-school or college group. If the right kids are involved, real enthusiasm can erupt.

The gimmick is to call on all new families, bearing gifts from retailers, along with public-service items like maps, brochures, and booklets on the area. Names of new arrivals can be obtained from city water departments or telephone companies.

Sponsor regular "newcomer meets" in the CBD so the families can get acquainted with each other and older residents.

WELCOME NEW RETAILERS

Lay the welcome mat out for new retailers as well, and make each new arrival feel a vital and wanted part of the CBD.

Gain goodwill and build a better community image by saying, "Hi, Neighbor," to new shopping centers if they locate in the community. Take ads saluting newcomers and announce there is

The Boulder, Colo., Chamber of Commerce makes all new businesses welcome by sending them this certificate and their first dollar of clear profit.

room for all. Offer newcomer bargains in a promotion geared to aid—not compete with—the new arrivals' grand opening events.

WELCOME COMMUNITY GROUPS

New local groups continue to form, and it takes considerable work before the community becomes aware of them. Help them along by holding welcome promotions for groups such as drum-and-bugle corps, dance groups, karate, judo, or yoga clubs.

Help a group get on sound financial footing by having them take over the store or a specific department, giving them a percentage of the sales. Urge them to come in their costumes. Stage an impromptu parade in the business district. Traffic will be built as relatives and friends of the group members come down.

Don't overlook older clubs, use similar ideas for these groups. Clubs register to be included, with names listed on a rotating basis.

CASH-REGISTER-RECEIPT GIMMICKS

Cash-register receipts can be used to assist local groups. Members and the public save receipts, to be returned for a rebate on the item the group wishes to purchase. This will get entire groups, and their friends and relatives, shopping.

SIDEWALK EXHIBITS

These continue to draw and will be even greater as people continue toward the outdoors for activity.

Invite collectors, pottery makers, mosaic-tile workers, basket weavers, photographers, painters, and others to participate in exhibits and displays. Set up outdoor shows on the sidewalks in the CBD, permitting local or area artists to work and sell their crafts there.

Encourage them to give instructions and to chat with passersby. Schedule demonstrations at given times.

In addition to the art groups, other interests also lend themselves well to sidewalk exhibits; for instance, Indian tribes can exhibit their culture, complete with dance performances. Youth groups will be anxious to show their skills; women's groups are often centered on specific hobbies, and students can participate.

MEET SPORTS FIGURES

Team support is always good. Have a "meet the player" promotion, and invite residents down to meet the team, be it college, high school, or Little League. Let team members circulate in the CBD, or assign one or two to each participating shop, where they can meet the public. Have them attired in uniforms to add atmosphere and interest.

Add a sales gimmick by offering to give a percent of the day's volume to provide new uniforms or equipment. Or use a free-ticket gimmick, giving tickets with each purchase to encourage local support.

AUTO SHOWS

Help dealers introduce new models, displaying them in the street so the public can get a real look.

Build family promotions around these, giving women and children something for which to shop while fathers look over the cars.

PET SHOWS

Many ideas can be built around pets, ranging from having local children exhibiting theirs to professional acts involving animals. You could have a professional in to give a workshop on the care of pets.

Perhaps some outdoor pet shows might be combined with a pet school, where children can receive instructions on how to train their pets.

FLEA MARKETS

These can be held in numerous ways. Hold a limited one by inviting area clubs to take assigned space and sell items as fund-making projects. Or throw one open to the public and let everyone get into the act. If necessary, make a small charge for each participant (this can offset publicity costs or go for a grand prize in a drawing); let them sell from their vehicles or from racks and tables they bring along.

Interest in the flea market will generate traffic and create extra store volume.

TRADING STAMPS

Stamps lend themselves to group promotions. Large items, like buses for youth groups, can be a winning factor. Arrange with stamp companies to give the high-cost item for a stipulated number of stamps. One retail group agreed that for 5,000 books they would provide a Scout troop with a bus. The Scouts helped spur customer interest by turning the parking areas and sidewalks into exhibits complete with powwows and other activities. They even set up children's nurseries and baby-sat while parents shopped.

If stores give various stamps, have the CBD information or promotional center serve as a stamp-swap service too.

A PERSONAL STAMP FOR THE CBD

Design a CBD stamp for all stores to give. Customers redeem books right at the stores or at a center in the CBD, with participating merchants contributing merchandise at cost and working out their own redemption value. This eliminates need to keep an assortment of stamp books; and customers will fill books faster and feel the stamp program more meaningful.

COMMUNITY THEATER

If the community has no amateur theater, the CBD can help start one. School drama coaches will help; so will radio and TV personnel. Almost every community has some would-be actors, and it is just a matter of getting them together.

Once organized, if they can be housed in the CBD (they'll need a practice hall and a place for storage, meetings), the group can be useful during promotions by dressing up and mingling with the crowd. They may also work up some 20- to 30-minute skits to be staged during specific events.

If a community theater group is already going, representatives of the CBD might meet with them and establish a relationship.

Give tickets to their performances as sales gimmicks; advertise in their programs; and help them find needed props, costumes, and other material.

REFRESHMENT STAND

Purchase or make a mobile trailer or concession stand on wheels, complete with CBD advertising on its side. This can be lent to community groups to use at their events, and it can also serve the CBD during outdoor promotion by providing snack items. And it can double as an information or promotion center during outdoor activity.

ICE-CREAM SOCIALS

Still fun—and CBDs with parklike atmosphere are ideal settings. If no natural park setting is available, create one with fake grass and artificial greens.

Retail groups should consider owning portable tables, folding chairs, ice-cream freezers, coffee urns, and equipment for making snack items to use when holding such events. Or let local groups provide the equipment and stage the event—with retailers profiting from increased traffic.

Try things to appeal to all tastes—an ice-cream social one time —a chicken barbeque another.

COMMUNITY ACTIVITY TIE-INS

These can be tied in with whatever activity is going on in the community. If the library is celebrating Children's Book Week, work with teachers and group leaders to stage contests or programs correlated with reading.

For adult groups, work with group leaders to tie in with their events, like historic home tours, garden shows, and other programs.

LECTURE LUNCHEONS

Hold a series of "be informed" lectures (but keep them short). Bring in authorities to participate. For the afternoon, design topics to appeal to women shoppers, with short question-answer periods. Provide refreshments, and let customers mingle and meet the speaker afterward. Hold outside in warm weather.

By the way, a microphone and PA system are things every swinging CBD organization should consider a must if it is to sponsor group activities.

ETHNIC ANGLES

Take advantage of the ethnic angle and build promotions around the origin of the community. Cooking demonstrations, old-time contests, arts and crafts, history and cultural items, all lend themselves to ethnic tie-in promotions.

DON'T FORGET THE ORPHANAGE

Don't overlook these often-forgotten ones. Take time out to do something for them. Include them in a children's event or make them honored guests at an event of their own. Women's groups will be happy to assist, providing the labor which may be needed, or transportation. Or work with a men's organization (a service or civic club) to take the children to a special community activity, like a circus, which they otherwise might miss.

ADOPT THE NEEDY

Adopt a needy child or group, either locally or overseas, by working through some of the national organizations which sponsor these programs. Stores can agree to underwrite basic support. Put up letters received from the person so customers and employees can read them. During the year, hold events to earn money which will be used to help the adoptee. This is a community-image project in which everyone can be involved, customers will soon be asking to be included.

FOUNTAINS

Install a fountain in the CBD to provide atmosphere—and good will.

Stage a "coin in the fountain" promotion, telling customers a specific goal has been set; that you hope to reach it by a specific date, with funds collected going to a specific project. On that date, clean the pool and turn over the funds.

During the year similar cleanings can be used for community goodwill purposes. Arrange cleanings so publicity can be gained, or make them part of a promotion, attracting the public to watch.

Perhaps hold a contest as to how much money will be cleaned from the pool, with customers guessing beforehand.

SCHOLARSHIPS

A CBD scholarship, especially in the field of retailing, will be a community service.

GIFTS TO COMMUNITY FACILITIES

Donations to local zoos, museums, animal shelters, and other facilities in the name of the CBD can also lend themselves to sales gimmicks.

Provide an exotic animal; hold a contest to pick its name, guess its weight, with the winner officially presenting it to the zoo in the name of the CBD. Hold a special presentation in the CBD so residents can meet the new arrival.

Similar promotions can be worked around items donated to museums, art galleries, and other public facilities.

YOUTH FAIRS

Help youth sell the results of its labor. Stage youth fairs where kids can sell items they have made or repaired.

If a local 4-H group holds an annual fair, and most do, CBD retailers should turn out in force, showing their support, purchasing steers and other livestock. Make a purchase or two in the name of the CBD and then hold a public feast.

SPONSORING SPORTS ACTIVITIES

It costs money to sponsor these, but they do build goodwill and reap publicity over a period of time. Retailers can aid in the publicity by mentioning teams and scores in their regular ads.

Sponsor a CBD team, providing attractive uniforms and equipment.

Or join in the activity by having a CBD team composed of store owners and management, and sponsoring another comprised of employees, with owners picking up the cost FOR BOTH. Imagine the fun and publicity if the two teams play each other in a match.

Interest and promotions can be built around rivalry between management and employees.

OPENING-DAY CEREMONIES

Throughout the year various community groups will hold opening-day activity for new buildings, projects, or programs. Get in on the action. Send congratulatory bouquets; run a congratulatory ad; offer specials; hold drawings for prizes; and have promotional activity emphasizing the activity and what it will mean to the community.

If necessary, schedule free bus or car rides to the opening, courtesy CBD.

USING RADIO AND TV TECHNIQUES

These can offer imaginative promotional gimmicks. Try a radio or TV talk show patterned after the late-night TV shows; or stage local talent programs. How about news-type programs sponsored by the CBD, or white-paper-type programs on local matters?

Spur interest by asking the viewing or listening audience to send in topic ideas, even take part in the program by a voting gimmick when questions are asked, from time to time, to get local response.

Let informality reign by originating the broadcast in a local restaurant or in a CBD store; keep new faces on the screen or air by changing participants frequently.

Originate the program over mid-morning coffee, in the CBD, inviting shoppers at random to participate. Sprinkle the program with special guests for added variety.

USE MEDIA MOBILE UNITS

These are good not only for advertising promotional activity in the CBD but because they themselves are an attraction. Many stations now have portable units, usually in a van or bus, so actual on-the-spot coverage can be given specific events. Have announcers get out and talk with the public, mentioning names of those at the event. This can be a drawing card to lure others downtown.

TV AUCTION

Use the television to sell merchandise without even opening the shops. Customers have the added benefit of shopping from home. Merchandise is shown on the screen, an item at a time. Each is numbered. Listeners have 15 minutes after the item is shown to phone in their bids, with the highest bidder announced. Customers stop in the store the next day to buy the items at the price they bid.

Have enough telephones available so all callers can get bids through.

The promotion can be used solely as a retail event or tied in with a local group, with a portion of the proceeds going to the group.

CLEANUP GIMMICKS

This can be repeated yearly. (Even monthly, but that might be overdoing it.) All that is needed are a few innovations and a catchy name each time. Announce what improvements will be made in the CBD and then urge residential areas to follow the lead on a group basis.

CBD projects might include putting awnings on all store fronts. If the same size and height, they add unity, but can provide individuality by being differently colored, for a rainbow effect.

Or invite a town down the highway to a contest. A group of cities did this, painting store fronts. The gimmick was that at noon all brushes used in City A were sent to City B, and vice versa, so that each city finished with the other city's brushes.

Instead of competing, cities within a ten- to 20-mile radius can join forces in similar promotions to arouse area interest and bring people from far-reaching areas into both communities. This can be the beginning of dual promotions in the future. Get carpenters, roofers, painters, electricians, and others to combine on a community repair job, with retailers supplying materials. Probably there is a children's home that needs a play area; a zoo which needs a new pen; or a fire station which needs an addition. Or build a new house for a needy family, using men from the construction trade as bosses for non-experienced residents who will want "in." Stores can supply materials and snacks at the site.

Contests among merchants can be staged, with an award to the one who does the most unique repair job of the year. Give a related prize to the resident who does the most to fix up his property.

CATER TO ALUMNI NOSTALGIA

Any time groups return to the community, they should be met with a welcome sign and old-fashioned hospitality.

Alumni, especially, have an interest in the community. Decorate store windows with school colors, old pictures, and mementos of the class which is returning. Old yearbooks should be dragged out and displayed along with newspaper clips from the graduation year. Extend a special invitation to them to return to the downtown for a special event.

TRADE SHOWS

Home shows, sports shows, yard and garden shows, all make for good group activity. Hold them in a CBD auditorium, armory, school, or wherever ample space is available.

When retailers join together to emphasize new products, customers can see a large variety of items at one time, under one roof, in an informal setting.

Demonstrations, contests, free literature (provide large shopping bags advertising the CBD so literature and giveaways can be carried easily), token gifts and samples, advertising, souvenir items, and entertainment (at specific or scheduled times) are all good gimmicks.

Fashion shows can be tied in with the theme to pull women customers—but don't forget to include sports attire for the entire family, as the informal setting will provide a good background for this category.

Have concession stands or booths available; consider customer-participation entertainment such as trout ponds, archery ranges, golf greens.

The success to this is in the large variety of participants. Open the show up—don't bar competition. Let all firms join in. This provides variety and helps spread costs, which are usually absorbed by selling booth space.

TRAVEL PROMOTIONS

Travel, vacations, recreation. These are the big key words in today's casual living, and shows featuring merchandise geared toward this field are usually well received.

Stores can join together. Apparel for traveling or vacation, luggage, boating, camping, automobile accessories, food preparation on the road or on vacation, ways to keep children amused when traveling—all are ideas which retailers can build into travel shows. Have travel-bureau personnel on hand to give out brochures and information.

Travel bureaus can also furnish posters, etc., for color. Invite an airline to send a chic stewardess to "tell it like it is" to fly high.

Hotel, motel, camping, or recreational businesses in the area may want to join in. Ask them.

GIVEAWAYS

These are good; if the prize is big enough a huge crowd can be drawn.

Lure customers to the CBD by giving away a costly gift (how about a thousand bucks?). One method is to choose the winning name by using the telephone book. Have a child from the audience draw a number out of a hat; if it is 16, for example, the 16th person listed in the book gets the prize—IF HE IS IN THE CROWD. Give winners several minutes to come forward. Then draw another number—repeat this several times.

Continue the event nightly, or weekly, until the prize is won. The gimmick is that the winner must be present to win—that will bring hopefuls downtown. Increase interest by adding more money each night or week that the prize goes unclaimed.

Or have the customers register their names in stores beforehand, perhaps over a 30-day period, and use these from which to draw. But the winner must be present to win, or else the promotion loses its pulling power.

FOREIGN THEMES

This is a magic word; and promotions featuring imports are easy, as many nice and quality items are available in a wide price range.

With the emphasis entirely on imports or foreign items, each store can feature a special item and/or country as its theme. Or choose one city or country and have all retailers zero in on it for impact. If possible, fly someone there as a grand prize winner.

Or fly someone to your city to add glitter, such as a Paris designer or model; perhaps a French chef.

Print your own money—it's legal if you don't try to duplicate actual currency. Include the name of the community and event, and the "auction bucks" will provide a lot of fun when used in promotions.

PROMOTE AMERICAN PRODUCTS

Plan a promotion, with each store offering specials made in the United States.

Add a novel twist by featuring some items made or produced in your own city or area, using special prices to lure people in.

BINGO-BUCKS

Each retailer places some merchandise in the street at a central location. Customers try to guess the exact retail cost of the entire lot. They note their decision on an entry blank to which they attach "bingo-bucks," in the same amount as their estimate.

Bingo-bucks are tokens distributed over a 15- to 30-day period beforehand, with one $10 bingo-buck given for each $1 purchase at participating stores. If the total merchandise on display is worth $450, a customer must have spent $45 locally during the previous period to enter that amount. Winner receives all items on display.

MUSICAL DISCOUNT

At intervals, blow a large horn or siren, or ring a bell, that can be heard throughout the CBD. All customers paying for merchandise at that time receive their purchase free or at a stipulated discount, depending on amount of item.

CREATING "BAD WEATHER" TRAFFIC

During slack periods that accompany snow storms, draw customers into the CBD by having a Snowflake Party. This must be put into action on the spur of the moment, so it must be pre-planned.

As snowflakes appear for the second or third day, announce on radio or TV that a Snowflake Party is in progress. All stores feature items at a "melting price" to entice customers. Announcements must state that the minute it stops snowing, prices return to normal. Offer coffee and rolls to those who brave the snow.

AIR TOURS

Many residents may never have had a bird's-eye view of their community. Arrange with a local airport for an air tour, with each trip lasting ten to 15 minutes.

THE WONDERFUL WORLD OF (YOUR TOWN)

Build a promotion around the old home town. Use advertisements, in-store displays, and gimmicks to push local products, industry, talent, artists, institutions, groups, schools, civic and community facilities into the limelight. Zero in on something different each week, or day, depending on length of event. The community will benefit from the image projected, and many will be surprised that their home town has so much to offer.

TAKING PRIDE IN THE COMMUNITY

No community can take pride in its past if residents have no knowledge of its history. With the mobile age, and people moving every few years, a large percentage of residents in any community are new. What is old hat to retailers who have long served the area is unknown to many of the customers.

Many communities do not have museums or active historical societies to promote knowledge of the area history. Retailers can enhance their image by taking on the project or starting a project with other groups. Retailers can provide display area; help with publicity and advertising; perhaps offer a central location for exhibits.

Themes like "We take pride in our community" or "From a proud past to the glorious future" can be used.

PROVIDE COMMUNITY INFORMATION

With today's fast pace, a host of information is gobbled up daily by everyone in the community. Retail groups and Chambers of Commerce are looked to as the central figures in providing this.

Make street maps available, with points of interest shown. Keep them current, updating every few years. Pertinent information either on the maps' reverse side or in a separate brochure should be available, and should include a brief historic resumé of the community; population figures; list of educational facilities; list of public facilities; church listing.

A more complete, atlas-type brochure could include store lists, bus routes, taxicab companies, civic, fraternal and service organizations, recreational sites, and perhaps a zoning map.

These can be given out at a CBD information center or by individual stores via racks. They should be available for new retail prospects, who will need such information, as well as for residents.

RETAIL INVOLVEMENT IN COMMUNITY PROJECTS

Frequently entire communities band together to provide recreational, educational, or other facilities. Retailers, both independently and as a group, can do much to improve their image by being in the forefront of these campaigns.

Typical is a Connecticut retail group which invested some $2,000 in a 35x80-foot parcel of land, which was turned over to the city for a playground.

COURTESY SERVICES

Every community needs courtesy services such as rest rooms, drinking fountains, pay telephone booths, often in areas other than the CBD. Retailers spearhead drives for these, even donate them in the name of the CBD.

ENCOURAGE COMPETITION

A major criticism frequently voiced by residents is that the retail element freezes out competition. This idea is damaging and every effort should be made to counter it.

Gimmicks include active campaigns, with publicity, encouraging new retail enterprise from outside; or encourage a home-grown one to sprout up.

CHAPTER
10

RX for Parking Ills

Parking, the menacing problem of the 'sixties, is still unsolved in many retail communities, and the 'seventies are expected to bring many innovations in this area.

Oftentimes costly solutions may be the only answer, with high-rise parking ramps, elaborate transit systems, or re-routing of traffic. By their very nature these must be community oriented, and because they will require extensive professional planning and engineering, they will be mentioned only briefly as possible gimmicks to be used.

The ideas in this chapter are primarily geared toward solutions retailers, or groups of retailers, can employ without requiring municipal or engineering involvement to any large extent.

Searching for Potential Parking Places

OFFICE BUILDINGS

Many are located in retail areas, with their own smaller parking lots. These firms usually are not open evenings or weekends, now the prime shopping time. Arrange to utilize these lots for customer shopping during the off hours of the firms involved.

REAR ALLEYS

Rear alleys can be utilized more. They can ease parking problems in a number of ways. Trucks unloading in front of stores and blocking vital parking spaces could unload in the rear—special loading doors or ramps may be needed. Deep alleys can be turned into parking spaces, with retailers banding together, creating park-like settings, and locating mini-parking lots behind their stores.

If rear alleys are converted to parking lots, remember that women and children shoppers like pleasant entrances and not dark corners. Add canopies, add greenery; install ample lighting.

DRIVE-INS AND REGULAR THEATERS

Often located in the retail area, or close to it, these have spacious lots, and many operate nights only. Arrange to use their facilities during daytime hours.

SCHOOLS AND CHURCHES

These are good sites for extra parking spaces, with most communities having them near retail areas. Arrange to use these lots when not in use by the church or school.

UTILITY FIRMS AND WAREHOUSES

Often near the business district, they have vast lots which probably could be used evenings and weekends.

RAZED PROPERTIES

Most retail areas have older homes or other dilapidated buildings which should be razed. Because the property is in the business or fringe area, it will be worth far more than its current use would make it seem. But, even so, retail groups will do well to purchase such properties before they are gobbled up and converted to other use. Benefits are two-fold: retail group-owned parking lots are provided and a blight area is removed.

CURB UP DRIVEWAYS

Unused driveways can be "curbed up" and converted to parking space. A quick walk through the business district may reveal several of these.

SIDE STREETS

Side streets adjacent to retail areas often contain sites which could be converted to parking. Perhaps this will involve purchasing and leveling an existing structure, but its location will be convenient for shoppers.

CHANGE PARKING FORMAT

Many communities still have wide streets, a carry-over from the old days. A change from parallel to angle parking will provide added space and not interfere with traffic flow.

WIDEN STREETS

There are many advantages to widening streets, even if it means narrowing sidewalks. It is frequently less expensive than buying off-street lots for parking; it distributes parking spaces evenly throughout the downtown area; if traffic loads get heavier, parking can be abolished in later years and the space used for other purposes, leaving the widened streets for greater traffic flow. In the meantime, angle parking can be offered.

ELIMINATE ''SPECIAL'' PARKING SPACES

Take a look at "special" on-street parking privileges. Are these posted or reserved areas really necessary? Often they are just offered as favors and can be eliminated.

SCHEDULE REPAIR WORK AFTER HOURS

Meet with city officials to arrange repair work after store hours. Such work snarls traffic during the day, removes valuable parking spaces. Early morning and evening hours may be suited for work on streets in the business area.

If day-only work is a must for city employees, stores can counter by closing during the day (keeping traffic down and helping crews finish their work faster). Stores can open extra early in the morning, and then hold hours again at night, during the improvement program. With gimmicks tossed in for added appeal, customers may be enticed to do their shopping earlier or later.

VACANT AUTOMOBILE AGENCIES

Many automobile dealers are moving to fringe areas where acres of property are available so they can spread out. Their former buildings in the retail district stand empty. Retailers can band together and gain tremendous parking and community-service space by purchasing these.

The garage itself can be converted to inside parking either for customers or retailers, getting their cars off the streets. This type of parking can pay its own way on a reserved-space basis. Outdoor lots, which were often part of the dealer's operation, may need little work to convert them to public parking lots.

Showroom areas in the garage, often airy and with floor-to-ceiling windows at the front, can be turned into downtown information centers, lounge areas, and meeting rooms for customers and public. Or they can become waiting areas for shuttle buses taking shoppers to parking lots on fringe areas.

FAIRGROUNDS AND FARMERS' MARKETS

Fairgrounds, farmers' market areas, and similar places even if still in operation near or in the business district, provide parking spaces which may be converted to public use during their off periods.

CONVERT OLD RAILROAD TERMINALS

Located in the heart of most business communities, many terminals are now empty or near deserted due to the decline of railroad services. Frequently the grounds can be rented and converted to parking areas. Old passenger terminals lend themselves well to retail-oriented information centers, waiting rooms, or lounge areas.

UNUSED ALLEYS

Most retail areas have municipally owned alleys which are seldom used. With cooperation from city officials, these can be taken over by an organized retail group and converted to mini-parking lots.

CITY AND COUNTY FACILITIES

These normally close at 5 p.m. and are frequently in the retail area, so an abundance of parking spaces is available for evening and weekend use. With the right approach municipal officials may be persuaded to allow this.

FACTORIES

Carry-overs from pre-zoning days, many industries are still found in the retail area or at its fringe. Frequently these are small and do not operate after 5 p.m. or on weekends. Their lots may be available to retailers.

Mass Transit

Multi-benefits can be gained if cars can be kept out of the retail area. Mini-buses, shuttle buses, mass-transit buses, monorail passenger trains are among methods which can be used to decrease demand for parking spaces in the core area and to eliminate or reduce traffic congestion.

Mass transit can handle swarms of downtown employees, customers, and clients. It slashes traffic congestion, especially during peak-hour loads, and cuts the need for parking.

Among ideas are:

SENIOR-CITIZEN BUSES

Help senior citizens shop by providing vans or mini-buses to their housing developments during specific hours (low traffic periods is one time). These people are usually slower, taking more time to shop, and their cars use space which would be turned over faster by younger shoppers. Mini-buses to serve them on specific days will reduce this added congestion, and it will also provide a service many elderly persons would welcome.

MINI-BUSES IN THE SHOPPING DISTRICT

Ease congestion by providing mini-buses touring the business area, moving shoppers from one end to another at low cost, thereby eliminating the need for them to use cars.

REJUVENATE THE OLD TROLLEY

If the trolley tracks are still in the streets, bring the trolley back as a method of moving people in the downtown area. Nostalgic, painted nicely, it can become an attraction on its own.

SHUTTLE FROM OUTLYING LOTS

Large lots on the outskirts of the community can be developed for retail parking if shuttle service is provided to taxi customers back and forth.

WORKINGMAN'S SHUTTLE

Use shuttle buses for working men to take them from outlying lots to downtown. With proper promotion, they will learn to enjoy the ride, for it will be inexpensive and as quick as trying to drive their own cars into the CBD.

Shopping centers with large parking lots often solve the parker's problem of getting to the store by having "shopper's trolleys" that make scheduled runs around the parking lots to pick up the shopper and later return them to their cars. (Courtesy of Fairchild Visuals)

EXECUTIVE SPECIAL

Run this bus from outlying parking areas or have it pick up businessmen at their homes. The same service can be provided after work, with one run made in the evening for those who work late.

This will give executives an opportunity to meet and discuss items of mutual interest without taking time from their busy days.

Add a touch of luxury to the buses, and businessmen will quickly prefer them. Included could be contoured seats, stereo music, twin seats facing each other so the men can play cards, vending machines for coffee and cold drinks, newspapers and magazines.

WORKING GALS' SPECIAL

Same as for the executive, but cater to gals working in the core area.

Mass Transit—Large-Scale Basis

Subway riding, which hit a low in many communities in the 'fifties, is on the upswing as traffic congestion and 5 p.m. snarls exasperate people, causing them to seek the speed, comfort, and ease of mass transit.

Monorails are becoming popular; and a host of other new ideas to speed mass transit will crop up as imaginative transportation officials, city officials, and retailers join forces to solve problems.

Getting the people back onto the buses seems to be the new trend.

The pendulum is swinging, and many are predicting mass transit will be the thing of the future.

PERSUADING THE PUBLIC

If mass transit is a real need in the community, begin the push by getting service, fraternal, women's, retail, business, municipal, school, church, and other concerned groups together to brainstorm ideas. Have professionals ready to explain what is available in the field.

The project will probably have to be on a municipal basis,

necessitating bond issues. Retailers can help pave the way by being influential in supporting and publicizing the merits of the system, which may meet taxpayer and voter resentment in some cases.

All facts should be presented—openly.

UPGRADE OLD BUS LINES

Frequently privately-operated bus lines are forced out of business. Many reasons are given, but often the retailers are guilty of not helping promote bus travel with validation plans, offering free rides as prizes, or riding the buses themselves.

Instead of allowing such services to close, retail groups can take them over. (See next two sections on how to make these attractive and how to promote them.)

DOUBLE-DECKER BUSES

These are appealing and carry more people than regular buses do.

SPECIAL TRAFFIC LANES

Mass transit must move quickly if it is to serve its purpose. Establish special lanes, eliminating traffic delays.

Or have streets which run parallel to the retail district turned into routes for buses only. This will eliminate much traffic on them (except for homeowners and their guests).

EXPRESS TRANSIT

Express buses going directly from specific residential areas to central core locations are speedy; they will lure riders during rush hours if the time-consuming stops at every corner are eliminated.

DESIGNATE BUS STOPS

A must in mass transit, those spots should be well marked and other vehicles prohibited from using them. This will improve traffic flow, aid transit, and increase pedestrian safety.

SPECIAL PROMOTION EXPRESS BUSES

During specific promotions, shoppers' express buses to specific suburban areas may be needed. Provide for a few specified stops—most women won't mind walking a block or two.

MONORAILS

Popular and worth investigating if the area is large enough to support one. Attractive elevated roadways for cars, buses, trucks, and pedestrians are definitely the "in" thing.

TUNNELS

In some larger cities, tunnels are becoming popular as a means of moving people. This is another area where a professional will be needed.

MULTI-LEVEL TRAFFIC

Traffic congestion problems in many downtown areas will probably best be solved, with professional help, by putting various kinds of traffic at various levels. As population increases, this will become a reality in many communities.

Vertical transportation—the up-and-down movement of people inside the core area—is adequately meeting the need in some areas.

If downtown has already become compact, shoppers and businessmen can only be served by getting maximum value out of costly land—development must go up into the air space above existing facilities. And/or down beneath them.

Stairways, ramps, elevators and escalators—second-floor rejuvenation: these are all part of the picture.

Because this type of development calls for firm structural planning, professionals are needed, along with co-operation of large groups of businessmen.

If accomplished, however, the entire program may be the needed attraction to spur activity in the retail center.

Mass Transit—Making It Attractive

Perhaps no other area relating to retailing is so bogged down in old myths as mass transit and its promotion. As with passenger trains, oftentimes retailers and mass-transit operators know little—and care less—about pleasing the customer.

Promoting riders, stimulating people to leave the car home and ride the bus—these are things on which retailers and mass-transit operators must concentrate if mass transit is to be used to alleviate parking ills.

KEEP BUSES CLEAN

Well-washed buses, inside and out, with clean windows and seats that have been dusted, will do much to keep customers riding.

PACKAGE RACKS

One frequent complaint about buses is the lack of space for packages. Ample racks should be provided.

MARK BUSES WELL

Nothing irritates a rider more than finding himself on the wrong bus. Printed schedules and maps posted at all bus stops are necessary.

One gimmick is to use colored lines on the maps with matching colored signs on the bus for quick passenger identification.

POST SCHEDULE CHANGES

Another gripe is that schedules are changed with little or no publicity. When schedules change, get the word out. Post new bus schedules immediately.

Restudy scheduling periodically. What was good ten years ago may not serve the public today.

TRANSFERS

These can pose real problems. Publicize transfer policy. Make studies periodically to insure that riders transferring do not have long waits and that buses involved arrive at the same location as close together as possible.

BOARDING POLICY

Avoid confusion at pick-up points with a firm "in the front door, out the back door" policy. Post this inside buses so customers know.

SCHEDULING IN THE SUBURBS

Some customers don't ride the bus because the walk to and from stops is impossible, especially with packages.

Updated studies and rescheduling are needed to alleviate this.

COMFORTABLE SEATING

Make certain seats are comfy and large enough for two persons.

AIR CONDITIONING

If extremely hot weather is a factor, air conditioning may be needed to keep people riding.

DRIVER COURTESY

A major complaint of riders is that drivers are discourteous and uncooperative. Train drivers in customer relations. A courteous driver may spell the difference between a successful run or one which customers reject.

KNOW THE DRIVER

Friendliness and warmth are generated if riders know their driver. Post signs including driver's picture and name at the front of the bus. Stir interest among riders by having "my favorite driver" contests.

GLAD YOU'RE RIDING

Customers feel welcome if drivers greet them with, "Glad you're riding with us today," as they board. A "welcome" sign on the bus also helps. Signs on the outside of the bus can urge others to "ride with us," listing reasons why: speed, low cost, no traffic congestion, relaxation, etc.

SHELTER AREAS

In the downtown core area, canopies can be used in spots where waiting is for short periods. This will provide shelter in inclement weather.

Where waiting may be longer (in parking lots on fringe areas or at major terminals where a number of buses arrive), permanent shelters are a must. These should be clean, well-lighted, and well ventilated, and should provide rest rooms. Air conditioning and stereo music will be welcome; vending machines may be profitable and provide customer service; drinking fountains are a must; having an assortment of magazines and newspapers available to riders will make the wait seem shorter. An ample supply of chairs should be available.

Auxiliary services could include pay telephones, postal drop box, a pay-box for public utility bills.

Shopping bags can be sold from self-service racks.

Use acoustic materials in construction to reduce noise and confusion.

Gimmicks to Promote Mass Transit

In areas where mass transit is new, considerable promotional gimmicks may be needed to offset resident opposition. Even those unopposed may have to be sold on its worth, as it isn't easy to break away from the family auto.

In areas where mass transit is already a reality, continued promotion will keep riders riding and attract new ones.

Retailers, who benefit greatly from mass transit, can do much to help promote it.

DUMMY PARKING TICKETS

Print make-believe parking tickets and put them on cars in the downtown area, telling drivers of the mass-transit system and its benefits. Include information regarding cost and routes, and stress relaxed riding while someone else does the driving.

ENCOURAGE OFF-HOUR TRAFFIC

Everyone loses when buses operate with few or no passengers, yet there are specific times when traffic will be low. Transit firms can reduce fares during these off hours to increase traffic.

Peg retail promotions toward customers during these hours, offering low prices for those who have used the transit. A ticket stub will identify riders.

DISCOUNT TICKET BOOKS

Encourage riders by selling books of tickets at reduced prices.

Stores can cooperate by giving these as gifts or prizes during promotions and by selling them for the transit firm, allowing customers to charge them on their store accounts.

FREE BUS TICKETS

Give free bus tickets to customers on certain days to encourage them to ride the bus.

RIDE-THE-BUS WEEK

Set aside a specific week to promote mass transit. Use a barrage of ads, with every store mentioning mass transit; have posters widely displayed; put up in-store and window displays; the mayor can issue a proclamation; public officials and retailers can ride the transit system and have this publicized.

FAMILY-FARE PLANS

Encourage the entire family to ride by selling tickets at reduced rates which are good for the entire family—perhaps on Saturdays or during evening hours.

MAGAZINE RACKS

Stock these on buses for rider use.

FREE RIDES

Use a validation plan, with clerks giving free tickets or chits to customers. Free rides should be used as gimmicks during heavy promotional periods as well as during low times.

TRADING STAMPS

If trading stamps are used, stores can generate transit interest by offering double stamps to customers showing transit stubs. Or they might give stamps with every book of tickets sold.

TIE IN RETAIL PROMOTIONS
WITH TRANSIT SYSTEM

During retail promotional activities, include the transit system. Example: at Christmas time Santa can make guest appearances on various runs, surprising riders.

LAUNCHING A TRANSIT SYSTEM—TRIAL RUNS

If a large transit system is to be launched, a trial period may be desirable. Arrange with schools during the summer to use their buses. This will reduce costs and give some indication of whether a transit system is needed and will be used.

Parking Meters—Necessary or Not

This is still a controversial subject, with some retail groups fighting to eliminate meters while others are insisting they be installed.

Some cities have eliminated them entirely and returned to free parking. Unfortunately, people often abuse this privilege. To combat this, some reverted to the old system of chalking tires; timed parking was instigated; fines were upped for overtime parking violators.

Chances are there will be no program which will please all retailers, businessmen, customers, and city officials.

The best approach is to have an unbiased study made of the problem, probably by an outside firm, to determine the best overall solution.

Gimmicks with a meter tie-in include:

FREE PARKING AT METERS

Retailers provide free parking by paying the city not to collect meter revenue. The retailers might use this method only during specific promotions. Meters can be covered with hoods; or in some communities city officials will cooperate by asking police officers not to check meters during specific promotional periods, such as holiday time.

When doing this, however, retailers should remember they are defeating the very purpose for which meters were installed—to make parking easy for those not staying for lengthy periods. Problems may also arise with some retailers or employees using the meters, thereby eliminating spaces.

METERED LOTS

Have short-time parking on streets to keep traffic moving, with long-time parking available in nearby metered lots.

STRICT ENFORCEMENT OF TRAFFIC AND METER RULES

If the community has restricted parking times or meters, rules should be strictly enforced—for everyone. The "guy who gets away with it," be it overtime parking or meter violations, hurts the downtown image: it annoys the public to see preferential treatment, and it is grossly unfair to those who obey regulations.

TEST PERIOD FOR METER ELIMINATION

Communities seriously opposed to meters can try a month-long test period to learn what customer reaction will be. In that length of time they will know if the city can stand the revenue loss; if store owners and employees are hogging parking spaces; if customers are abiding by posted parking-time limits; if problems are erupting because some people park for lengthy periods with little parking-space turnover available.

Parking Meter Gimmicks

HONOR BOXES

Post time limits; parkers are on their honor to put their change in boxes, several of which can be located in each block.

PARKING COINS

Most customers have experienced the joy of finally finding a parking space only to be dismayed to find they have no change. Most have also experienced the clerk who grudgingly changes a bill for parking meter coins.

One retailer, after being subjected to such discourteous treatment, did something about it. He posted a sign stating, "We have plenty of parking coins—please come in and feel welcome to get parking-meter change," in his window.

Instruct clerks regarding courteous handling of requests for change.

FISHBOWL OF COINS

Place fishbowls of coins on counters in front of stores with signs saying, "Caught without a cent? Help yourself to coins for parking." Most customers will take only what is needed—many will even pay the bowl back later. This shows trust in the public, provides a needed service, and creates goodwill.

TIME CLOCKS FOR TICKETS

One retail group felt it wrong for persons who made an honest effort to return to their parked cars but arrived a few minutes late to pay fines.

The group purchased time clocks. Anyone receiving a ticket could have it stamped by a clock. If less than 15 minutes had elapsed from time the ticket was issued, the ticket was excused.

COURTESY BOXES FOR TICKETS

Scatter these throughout the core area, making it convenient for shoppers to pay their tickets immediately without having to visit police headquarters.

Some cities even have reduced rates for tickets paid immediately, like 25¢ if paid within an hour and $1 or $2 if paid after that.

COLOR-CODE METERS

At the 1962 International Municipal Parking Congress a resolution was passed calling for uniform colors to designate time limits on parking meters. All cities were asked to follow the official color code. If your community doesn't, retailers should request the code be enforced, providing uniformity with other cities.

The code is as follows: 15 minutes, copper; 30 minutes, yellow; 60 minutes, green; 90 minutes, blue; two hours, silver; four hours and over, brown.

Publicity of the color code will permit shoppers to spot the type of meter they want in a hurry. Perhaps only two colors will be needed in many communities. If they are color coded, they can be intermingled. An example would be to have all two-hour parking except for the end meters in each block, which would be 15-minute ones, for those needing only short-time parking. This will open up several spaces in each block frequently, and the customers will quickly spot them.

FREE PARKING NIGHTS AND SUNDAYS

Many communities give free parking at meters on nights and Sundays, especially if traffic is slow on those days and finding spaces is no problem.

Others offer free parking on Saturdays or other specific days which are slow for retailers, to entice customers on that day and reduce traffic on other heavy-traffic days. Retailers can cooperate by staging promotions on these days.

RETAILERS PAY FOR OVERTIME PARKING

Retailers drastically opposed to meters or customers having to pay overtime parking tickets can have the retail group pick up the ticket costs. This can backfire, however, as many customers may take advantage of the policy, resulting in a slow rate of turnover of parking spots.

PLUGGING THE METER

Have clerks in each store watch meters in front of the shop. When the violation flag goes up, a clerk runs out and puts a coin in. He also puts a small notice under the windshield wiper, saying that the retail organization saved the parker from getting a ticket, and that the driver can repay it by placing a coin in the box located in each block.

Retailers doing this, however, must remember that some shoppers may soon learn they won't get tickets, so they won't be in a hurry to move on. It can eliminate the very thing meters were meant to do—provide parking places. If the meters take pennies, one or two could be used, so only a short period of grace is provided. This courtesy will be appreciated by customers who tried to make their meter deadline; yet it won't permit any to take undue advantage of the gimmick.

Yes, Virginia—Retailers Are Guilty, Too

Unfortunately, most studies regarding parking meters indicate that retailers and their employees are among the big offenders, guilty of hogging spaces in the downtown area. One community found that 60 percent of the spaces on its main street were taken over daily by owners and employees.

Often retailers permit suppliers to use public parking spaces in front of their shops for loading and unloading purposes, thereby restricting the spaces for customer and public use.

Gimmicks which can be used to eliminate complaints against retailers include:

EMPLOYEE LOTS

Provide lots away from the downtown area for owners, management, and employees. Arrange to have one or two persons drive others from the lot to the store in the morning and at closing.

SHUTTLE-BUS CHIT

Provide employees with chits for riding shuttle buses from outlying parking lots to downtown areas.

OFF-STREET PARKING AWAY FROM CORE AREA

Encourage management and employees to park several blocks from the core area. Residential areas on the fringe offer day-long parking spaces which are seldom used.

RIDE THE TRANSIT

Management can lead the way toward community support of transit systems by riding the buses themselves and encouraging employees to do so.

CAR POOLS

These reduce the influx of vehicles into the downtown area. Pools can be worked out among employees of several neighboring stores. Oftentimes a general meeting may be needed to determine who lives where and to promote the carpool concept among workers. Management and owners aren't immune, but should lead the way and participate.

COMPUTER MATCHING SERVICE

Launch the car pool with a whammie—bring in a computer to match together commuters from the same area who could share rides.

Parking-Lot Gimmicks

Just as mass transit has frequently been rejected by the public, so have some parking lots. Frequently for the same reasons: inconvenience, dirt, poor lighting, expense, or because the public isn't aware of their existence.

Below are gimmicks which can be employed in the development and promotion of lots.

FORM A CORPORATION

Providing a parking lot is frequently too costly and too large a project for a small store. The answer is for a number of stores to get together or for the retail group as a whole to sponsor a program designed to provide lots in the business district.

Form a downtown parking corporation with retailers buying stock; financing lots, garages, and shuttle buses if needed. Profits can be plowed back into more lots until ample parking is provided, after which the incorporators begin getting their investments back.

Give some thought to working out details on a benefit-assessment basis, designed to provide parking lots with each retailer paying his share. Under this assessment method, retailers pay in proportion to the benefit they will receive. It may be necessary, if some refuse to cooperate, to reserve a lot for customers of specific stores only.

SOMETIMES IT PAYS TO
TURN DOWN MUNICIPAL HELP

While often desirable, municipal help is sometimes best avoided. With the many shopping centers on the scene, providing their own lots at their own expense, CBD retailers should be prepared for taxpayer opposition if the municipality is asked to use tax dollars to provide parking for CBD customers. Sometimes the entire retail image can be tarnished by a quarrel over this.

LOTS CAN PAY THEIR OWN WAY

Frequently the retail group will need its investment back so more land can be acquired for added lots in all core areas. This can be done by charging for parking, either with paid attendants or by installing meters on lots.

If municipalities develop the lots, taxpayer criticism can be reduced if meters are installed and the lot pays its own way.

PARKING LOT REJECTION—WHY

One small community experienced customer rejection of its lot, although it was but a block off the business district. A study revealed the lot was near a light industrial area; it was poorly lit; sidewalks were cracked and bad; the land was low, with puddles of water often forming. When these were corrected, customers began using the lot.

USE COLORS TO LEAD THE WAY

Develop a program of colored signs or walkways to lead shoppers to parking lots. One community uses a purple "P" to lead the way. People realize, when they see the purple "P" sign, that the lot is a public one.

Signs listing specific parking lane numbers and lot numbers will help shoppers locate their cars quickly.

SELF-SERVICE LOTS

If free parking is offered, no attendant is needed. Even if meters are used, customers can be taught to protect themselves in self-service lots. Signs should tell them to lock their cars.

Benefits of self-service lots are multiple, and retailers should consider them. Among them are: customers can get in and out faster by parking cars themselves than if they must wait for an attendant; operating cost is less; only the driver touches his car; drivers may lock their cars, whereas in attended lots they often can't; customers aren't affected by closing times; the lot operator has less responsibility for accidents or damage if customers drive their own cars.

LARGE SPACES

Although added cars can be handled by skimping on space size, studies indicate women and novice drivers shy away from lots where they might have difficulty entering and leaving. There are also more accidents reported in such lots.

ATTENDANT COURTESY

If attendants are used they should be well trained in how to treat customers courteously. Lack of this is a frequent shopper complaint.

BEAUTIFY LOTS

With parking facilities now occupying a large portion of all downtown land, they are prominent and exert an effect on the overall appearance of the retail area. Eyesores are not only ugly to behold, but they downgrade the entire area. Parkers reject them.

Beautify lots with good landscaping, paving, drainage, and lighting, and with painting of adjacent walls. Plantings can provide a park-like appearance. Provide trash containers to reduce litter.

If lots are privately owned and owners are unco-operative, work with city officials to pass and enforce ordinances restricting nuisances in the community.

PROTECT PARKING LOTS

Frequently municipally-owned lots, already in the business area, are threatened by municipal development. One community found city officials about to replace a parking lot with a new police building.

Prevent this by urging that such developments, which add to congestion, be placed on fringe areas. The retail group can pay fair market value to the city to keep a lot at their disposal, thereby providing funds for the city to purchase land elsewhere.

WALKIE-TALKIES FOR ATTENDANTS

If the lot is huge and attendants used, equip them with walkie-talkies so they can keep in touch, eliminating lengthy waits at the gate by customers.

Safety patrols in parking areas can guard against thefts as well as parking mishaps. The patrol car has a 2-way radio that is hooked up to the police department. (Courtesy of Fairchild Visuals)

PARKING-LOT SHELTERS

If lots are large and there are waits for attendants to return cars, provide canopy shelters for those waiting.

POST SIGNS ON LOTS WHEN FULL

Lots which are full should have signs indicating this.

If attendants are used, they can post the sign; if metered, an automatic gate can be used, the gate closing when the lot is full. Equipment especially designed for this is available, complete with automatic coin changers to activate the gate when the lot has spaces available.

POST RATES

Every parking lot which is not free, whether attendant operated or self–service, should have large signs clearly indicating rates.

PARKING-LOT MAPS

Every map of the city which is distributed by the retail group or Chamber of Commerce should indicate parking-lot locations. Consider printing maps indicating parking lots only, so they can be quickly spotted.

Such maps should be included in welcome packets for newcomers and should be available when large groups of people are expected, like conventions.

Promote parking lots periodically, by printing and distributing posters showing their locations and by running maps in newspaper ads.

If the lots are on one-way streets, this should be indicated on maps so drivers will be aware of proper routine.

PRIVATELY-OWNED LOTS

These are frequently the best answer to parking needs. Business operates parking lots on a profit-making basis.

Firms operating parking lots should receive full cooperation from the retail segment, which can offer free parking passes as prizes and gifts to help the lot succeed.

Complaints about the lot, which will be heard by retailers, should be passed on to owners and management so they can be corrected.

Other Parking-lot Locations

The fringe area isn't the only place where parking lots can spring up.

A survey of the core area may show a number of novel spots which can be developed for parking. Most of these will require professional planning and engineering and costly construction; but they may be worth the effort, for with a little imagination a parking lot can become an attraction for an area.

Ideas include:

OVER-THE-RIVER PARKING

One community, which grew up along both sides of a river, built a lot partially over the river, near a footbridge. It now unites both sides of the downtown.

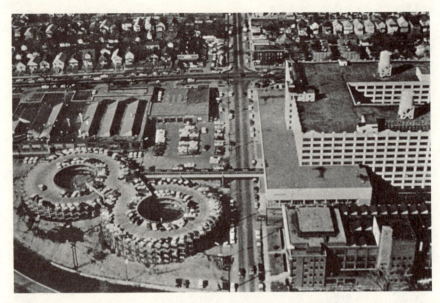

Multi-level parking is one way of solving the ever-increasing parking problem. Wards, Kansas City, Mo., handled this problem with a figure 8 parking structure. (Courtesy of Fairchild Visuals)

TRY A BARGE OR FERRY BOAT

If a river flows near the downtown, try a barge or ferry boat, which can be docked and used for parking.

DOUBLE DECKING THE STREET

Elevated parking lots over streets are new concepts in parking; some communities lend themselves well to this.

BASEMENTS

Most older retail communities have unused basement or cellar areas which can be converted. Ideally located in the core area, the cellars can be joined, and huge parking complexes developed.

ROOFTOPS

Just as basements lend themselves to parking lots, so do rooftops.

Again, engineering and planning are needed, with the project best handled on a group basis.

MULTI-STORY RAMPS

These permit mass parking on a limited amount of ground. Lift systems carry cars to various levels. Some plans include small stores and service outlets on the ground level. Whether these will be closed or open deck depends on the community and its preference.

These can be attended, self-service, even metered.

INNER-OUTER PARKING ZONES

An inner parking zone is for limited-time parking, metered, within the core area, with limits from 15 minutes to two hours.

Form an outer zone, including lots, ramps, etc., with free or reduced rates, on the fringe area, for longer parking periods.

Parking Validation Programs

Parking validation plans are common in many communities whether lots are city, retailer, or privately owned.

Such free parking lends itself well to retail promotions and gimmicks. Among those which can be used are:

PARKING STAMP

Good at any lot cooperating, and given uniformly by members of the retail group to customers making purchases in participating stores. Customers have their receipts stamped when they make purchases. These are given the lot attendant, and the retailer later redeems the stamp from the operator.

SHARED VALIDATION

So one store won't pay major cost of validation while customers shop in other stores, too, some communities work a shared validation. If one merchant stamps the parking ticket, the driver gets a 25-cent rebate; if a second store stamps it, he gets 35 cents off; and so on. The sliding scale arrangement is worked out among retailers and lot owners. Stores involved divide total costs on redemption.

Eliminating Traffic Congestion

There are a number of miscellaneous ideas designed to ease parking problems.
Included are:

MIXED-MODE TRANSPORTATION CENTER

One community decided to have a central transportation center for all forms of mass transit. They leased a former railroad terminal for an area passenger service; buses, rental cars, shuttle and mini-buses all make their headquarters there. Also incorporated was a downtown helicopter service.

GROUP WAREHOUSING

Eliminate congestion in downtown areas by mass warehousing for retailers on the fringe area or in one building to serve all. Semi-trailers do not congest the business district; smaller delivery trucks transport merchandise from the warehouse to various stores, as needed.

BYPASS TRUCK TRAFFIC

Much of the auto and truck traffic passing through retail areas does not have the downtown as origin or destination. Remove that traffic with a bypass route. This will also make parking at meters easier.

LET THE PUBLIC HELP

Housewives, college students, and the man who carries his lunch bucket often can come up with ideas which far surpass those of professionals. Bring these ideas to light by staging a contest and offering prizes for the best ideas on how to solve parking problems, gain parking spaces, and reduce traffic congestion.

BICYCLE RACKS AND MINI-BIKE PARKING

Urge shoppers, especially those who need pick-up items only, to make the switch from car to bike. Selling points include less cost, no air pollution, good exercise, an opportunity to enjoy the great outdoors. But make it easy for him: provide bicycle racks in the shopping area; a mini-bike parking lot. Include motorcycles here—frequently these take an entire parking spot when they need much less. Mini-bike parking areas can be located in small spaces but make them attractive and well lighted—and add a touch of green.

ENCOURAGE MAIL AND PHONE ORDERS

Get the message out to customers that mail and phone orders are welcome. Use a massive "shop at home" campaign. While this will eliminate some impulse sales, it will also help relieve congestion and parking problems. Most of these customers probably have specific needs and would not have lingered to shop anyhow. Some stores already have personal shoppers who answer these calls and then take responsibility for the items being delivered to the customer.

SHOPPING BAGS CAN ADVERTISE PARKING LOTS

Bags used by retailers to package merchandise can be imprinted with maps showing parking lots and giving mass-transit information, including bus schedules. This will acquaint customers with the facilities. Cost is reduced if the bags are purchased on a mass basis.

SUBSIDIZE THOSE WHO KEEP CARS OUT OF THE CORE AREA

Campaign to get customers to leave cars at home or to park in fringe-area lots. One retail group has stores stamp parking-lot passes for lots located outside the core area, with the retail group picking up the charge. They give credit slips for 25 cents to those who turn in used halves of bus tickets which brought them downtown; for elderly or handicapped persons, they pay a portion of the taxi fare when presented with a taxi pass.

CHAPTER
11

ABC's of Customer Service

Among frequently heard complaints in this era of mass merchandising is the lack of service. This runs the gamut from lack of service in appliance repairs to lack of service at the sales counter.

Ideas include:

EMPLOYEE COURTESY

Impress on employees that they are there to serve customers; that is their uppermost task, and it comes before employee conversations or preferences.

Taking time to help a customer is one service stores must retain to remain successful.

JUST BROWSING

Just as some persons will require help, others don't want it. Self-service has encouraged browsing, and many prefer the informality of this. One store gives buttons at the entrance which read, "I'm just browsing". Customers pin these on when they want to be left alone.

INFORMATIONAL CHARTS

Post at entrances, elevators, and lounge areas so customers know where to look for various departments and services.

Numbered entrances, such as this Arcade 5 sign, will be an aid to shoppers using stores or shopping entrances with multiple entrances. Similar signs located inside will help shoppers locate the right exit.

EMPLOYEE KNOWLEDGE OF STORE

All employees should know what items are sold in their and other departments. Too frequently customers are told, "We don't stock that", when it is available several counters away.

Stretch this: have employees acquaint themselves with stores in the retail district so customers aren't sent out of town to shop.

CUSTOMER COMPLAINT BOX

Keep in close touch with customer likes and dislikes. Have a complaint box available, with supply of note paper and pencils, so customers can write down gripes and suggestions. The cards can be read at weekly training sessions—if name and address is included a personal reply may be in order. Encourage such customer suggestions by offering a prize for the best one turned in each month.

Publicize complaints which resulted in innovations in merchan-

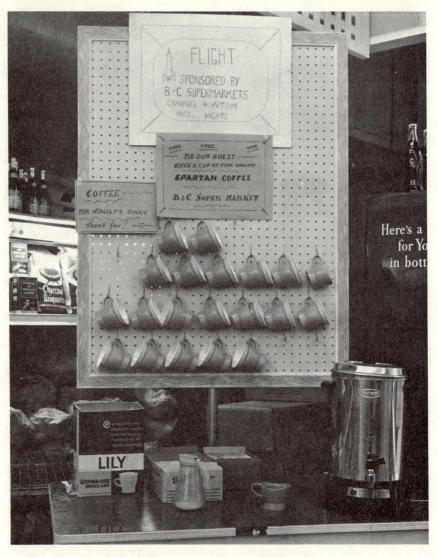

Just a simple free coffee counter like this will handle this courtesy service.

dising techniques or better customer service. This way customers will feel they play a vital role in the store's operation.

HOT-LINE TELPHONE

One retailer installed a hot-line telephone and connected it from the selling area directly to his office. The phone was for customer

A centrally located main-floor meeting area provides a place to relax while shopping, as well as an area for meeting friends. (Courtesy of Fairchild Visuals)

use in reporting complaints. This showed customers he really cared and put them in immediate touch either with him or with top management officials.

MAIL AND WRAP

See chapters five and six for details on this important service.

PACKAGE WITH CARE

Insure that customers are able to get their purchases home without breakage. Pack items in sufficient wrapping and in bags strong enough so bottoms won't tear out.

Use double bags if needed; have strong string and handles available so customers can carry boxes with ease.

CAREFUL WITH THE MARKING PENS

Another complaint customers have is due to the widespread use of ballpoint pens at the cash register. Frequently sales tickets are

We have you covered from your door to our store.

Two climate-controlled crosswalks bridge the new adjoining East Lansing parking ramp and Jacobson's. By parking on the third or fourth levels, you can walk directly into Jacobson's new location.

Jacobson's

E. Grand River at Charles East Lansing

Customer services such as covered entrances, climate-controlled crosswalk bridges and store-owned parking ramps can form the basis of a small-ad campaign.

tucked into packages containing delicate materials or apparel, with the ink rubbing off onto the merchandise. Or the clerk may be careless and mark the garment while she holds the pen during packaging; or a glob of the ink may be smeared on the counter and then rubbed onto merchandise.

DEMONSTRATIONS WITHOUT FUMBLING

Frequently customers request simple demonstrations on how an item works, only to find the clerk doesn't know how to operate the

A convenience many large stores offer is the in-store box office where one can purchase theater tickets while shopping. (Courtesy of Fairchild Visuals)

Providing a mobile shopping unit that travels to the customer periodically is a customer service still being practiced in more rural under-stored areas. (Courtesy of Fairchild Visuals)

gadget. Training for this should be mandatory; all clerks should acquaint themselves with new merchandise so they don't fumble with it while showing it to customers.

BULLETIN BOARDS FOR PUBLIC NOTICES

These are very popular, especially in stores which encourage browsing or which provide coffee or lounge areas for customer breaks. Customers can post notices on them, and stores as well—such notices are sure to receive attention.

Assign one staff member to watch the board, taking off notices after they have been up a week or so, and being responsible for its overall appearance.

COURTESY COUNTERS

Just what the name implies—counters where customers can seek information, obtain adjustments, get change, return items.

LOUNGE AREAS

Customers like to freshen up; they also need rest-room facilities.

One Virginia store offered individual booths in which customers could enjoy all the delights of a private bathroom, including shower. After a visit to the booth, tired patrons were in a better mood for shopping.

Another store installed a "sartorial parlor," where customers can find needle and thread to replace a missing button, mend a ripped seam, remove a stain, or handle any of the numerous other needs which may arise.

COFFEE SHOPS

If no coffee shop can be provided, use vending machines.

Or set up coffee on a small table, with customers informally pouring their own, and serving themselves rolls (which may be placed under a transparent cover). All that's needed beyond this is a cup in which they can put a nominal payment.

PUBLIC TELEPHONES

In a small store, customers can be allowed to use the store phone. Larger stores can install courtesy phone booths or pay booths.

FREE PHONE CALLS FROM SUBURBS

Stores which serve a large metropolitan area or which have customers in a number of outlying suburbs can arrange with the telephone company to have special numbers which customers can use for toll-free calls.

FAMILY-ORIENTED SERVICES

Most housewives cannot shop alone all the time. Small children frequently accompany them. Often entire families shop together. Their needs include snack items, telephones, lounge areas, and small play areas, which can range from segregated areas to a novel chair or paid kiddie ride at the front of the store.

RETURNS

Most retailers abhor returns, but they are a necessity. Firm policy on returns sometimes must bend to accommodate unusual situations. Customer courtesy is important on return items, as poor public relations can result if the return is not accomplished easily and pleasantly with customer satisfaction.

HEATED SIDEWALKS

If the store is located in a severe weather area, heated sidewalks will provide greater ease in walking, elimination of shoveling, and reduction in accidents; the sidewalk itself can be an attraction if it is the first in the community.

WEEKLY ACTIVITY GUIDE

Retailers as a group or independently can sponsor an activity column in the local paper. Area clubs merely phone in their activity reports directly to the paper. For added impact, clip the listing and post it on bulletin boards in stores.

STORE WINDOWS FOR COMMUNITY POSTERS

Store windows can be used for signs and posters listing community events. If the store is in a prime location, it may want to make a sign board for community use.

Urge club members to make their signs attractive and readable, and establish a policy wherein they will be put up only one week before the program to avoid window clutter. Have a clerk responsible for making certain signs are removed immediately after the event.

SPEAKERS' BUREAU

Retailers can provide a community service and get their message across by providing a speakers' bureau. Retailers with speaking ability can take on a host of subjects vital to the retail segment and its relationship to the community. Clubs and organizations in every community require a large number of speakers each year. Assistance from retailers in filling this need will be welcome.

Retailers who belong to other organizations which have speakers available should get that information to the central retail bureau headquarters, so it too can be disseminated to the community.

REPAIR SERVICE

Last—but not least—is repair service. Anything that is breakable should be serviced. If stores don't offer the service, they should arrange for the return of the product to the manufacturer and take reponsibility to make certain lengthy delays are not experienced by customers.

Stores with service departments can provide well-trained staff, with updated training as products change.

Stores can group together, providing one repair service to handle all needs, each paying a percentage.

Another gimmick is to encourage a local repair business to handle store service as well as that of the public. Stores can then use this firm to handle their repair needs, eliminating need to staff and operate their own departments.

An added gimmick is to change the policy of servicing only what the store sells, and service all merchandise, thereby winning customers. People move frequently, and it is often impossible to take an appliance back to where it was purchased. In a new community, the need for repair service is often one of the first to arise; the customer will undoubtedly buy large items from the firm that services her, shunning an unco-operative retailer who refuses to assist her.

CHAPTER

12

The New Selling Day: Up to 24 Hours

Unfortunately, few retail districts have been able to agree on uniform store hours. Even stores in many shopping centers open and close at different times, to the confusion and dismay of customers.

The difference of opinion over hours will probably never be amicably resolved, but there are a number of gimmicks which can be employed to keep customers informed.

Catering to customers by remaining open when it is most convenient for them to shop is mandatory now. What once was the traditional Friday night shopping spree for some families is no more. In their quest to serve people, retailers long since began holding special night-time events during the week. "Marathons," "sella-thons," "all-night sales," "night-owl sales," and other special-hour events bloomed. These proved so successful in the 'sixties that for many stores they no longer are special hours but regular ones, meaning other gimmicks have to be employed to lengthen or expand hours.

Special events of three or four hours on specific nights are still popular; so are some of the extreme 15-, 24,- 36-, and 72-hour marathons.

Given catchy names, many of these promotions use stars, the moon, comets, and similar objects related to the night as decorations.

Gimmicks revolving around store hours include:

PUBLISHING OF UNIFORM HOURS

Retailers who do agree on hours can get their message out by including hours in ads, by displaying posters listing co-operating merchants and the hours they will be open.

PUBLISH INDIVIDUAL HOURS

If no uniformity in hours exists, each retailer can publish his own hours in ads.

NIGHT SHOPPING

Many stores are now open seven nights weekly, closing shop at 9 or 10 p.m. These hours should be stressed in store ads. Stores should be well lighted so shoppers can see that they are open.

MIDNIGHT MADNESS—OTHER NIGHTTIME GIMMICKS

A male clerk wearing pajamas, with contests centered around how long he can stay awake, continues to be good. Other ideas include low prices on specific items at certain hours throughout the night to keep customers coming. Or advertise that throughout the night great bargains will be offered impromptu—those present can take advantage of these.

Coffee and other snacks are almost a necessity in these nighttime promotions.

Use radio and television to build interest on the night involved— perhaps broadcast direct from the store so listeners and viewers will be attracted.

CINDERELLA PROMOTION

Dress female clerks in ball gowns and other formal attire; use pumpkin coaches for decorations. Pick a store Cinderella at midnight from among shoppers and shower her with gifts.

BREAKFAST ON US

Sponsor an all-night event, giving gifts each hour and offering better bargains as the night progresses. Serve early morning breakfast at 5 a.m. to those still there; then close the store at 6 a.m. and give the clerks the day off.

72-HOUR MARATHON

Offer a large gift to the customer who finds a clerk asleep during this lengthy program. Dress salesmen in nightshirts; use radio spots and TV, originating broadcasts from the store. Entire groups of people will come to join the fun if late-night snacks and scheduled entertainment are used to liven the event.

13-HOUR SALE

Especially good on Friday the 13th. You simply add an additional 13 hours of selling time or keep the store open a total of 13 hours. Use gimmicks and contests based on superstitions. Construct a 13-hour clock to use for contests; for instance, every time the hand hits 13, an alarm rings, a numbered wheel is spun and the customer holding the winning number receives a prize.

MAN IN THE WINDOW

A real attention-getter: a salesman actually lives in the window for a week, making sales after the store is closed. This is especially appealing in close-knit areas as word-of-mouth publicity will spread. Use heavy radio and TV broadcasting publicity with the announcer wondering periodically, . . . "what Jim down at Sandy's place is doing about now."

"Even our windows are good enough to live in" is a possible slogan.

Tie in with a nearby restaurant to serve the "window man" his meals, or with the popular space program, designing the window to represent a space capsule and having the clerk live on space foods.

ROUND-THE-CLOCK SALE

Remain open around the clock, putting a new item, at a greatly reduced price, up for sale one hour at a time. Best buys come late at night and in the wee hours of morning.

30-MINUTE SPECIALS

Offer large reductions on specials every 30 minutes. From 9 p.m. until midnight lock the door for 30-minute periods so only those already inside may partake of specials, which have been announced over a loudspeaker.

$5-TO-$1 MIDNIGHT SALE

Start at 4 p.m. with a large item offered for sale at $5. All those who intend to buy it must have dropped their names into a box by 4 p.m. A winner's name is drawn and, if the winner is in the store, he may buy the item for $5. If he is not present, another name is drawn.

Two hours later, at 6 p.m., a $4 sale is made in the same manner; a $3 sale at 8 p.m.; $2 at 10 p.m., and at midnight a lucky person can buy a large item for $1 if he is present.

All names are removed from the jar between drawings, so people must remain in the store during the evening event to re-register.

EARLY-BIRD HOURS

Just as the nighttime can attract shoppers, so can the early morning hours, especially if the gimmicks are unusual and the bargains good. Open early on a specific day; serve coffee, rolls; give out free morning papers. This can be turned into prime shopping time for those employed in the retail area who can't get away from their jobs during normal hours.

SUNDAY SALES

"Never on Sunday" may have been the theme song years back, but the 1960s changed all that. Sunday has become just another shopping day for countless customers. Many retailers report that this has become so successful they no longer use special gimmicks as stimulants.

Nevertheless, there are some elements about Sunday shopping that retailers can promote. Sunday is frequently a time of family-oriented activity, so make it relaxing and include all members. This is a good time for demonstrations on items in which father may be interested.

Make shopping on Sunday fun by playing little games in the store. For example, lights at certain counters can have colored bulbs, and at specific times an announcer can say that for the next ten minutes everything at the counter with the flashing light is reduced 25 percent.

Tie in the children by offering five-cent bags of popcorn (or other items) for 15 minute periods at the check-out counter.

Any game-type gimmick which adds fun to the afternoon can cause excitement.

Teen activity can also be used to pull youthful shoppers.

BE THE FIRST—STAY OPEN ALL NIGHT

Just as this chapter was being written it finally happened. A chain store in a nearby community announced its three branches would start staying open 24 hours daily. News stories included photos of a well-lit shop at night.

No longer will marathons and all-night events be special as the trend grows. Instead, retailers will have to hold special promotions and employ special gimmicks to entice customers during the wee morning hours.

This apparently will be one of the retail challenges of the coming decade.

CHAPTER
13

Turning the Clearance into a Store Plus

Every store needs a good clearance sale now and then to rid itself of leftover stock. Markdowns are inevitable if the merchandise is to be moved. When these sales are held can only be decided by the individual retailer, but surely when shelves are overflowing and new merchandise is arriving, the time is ripe.

Many stores report one or two large clearance efforts each year keep inventory in line. January and June have traditionally been considered good, but times are changing. Some firms report August and September are now prime months, especially for moving leftover summer stock.

Local circumstances must be given consideration in picking a sale date. If customers go south early in January, the clearance sales could be held early so spring items can be featured before they leave; but bear in mind that many remain behind; they will continue needing winter things, so don't clear everything out.

If weather remains nice well into the fall, summer items may sell at regular price without clearance. If a cold snap hits early, a clearance of summer items should probably follow, for, once woolens have been taken from the mothballs, most families will continue wearing them.

Numerous benefits besides inventory reduction are derived from store-wide clearances. The new season can be met head-on with new merchandise. There is no overlap period with both old and new items on the shelves.

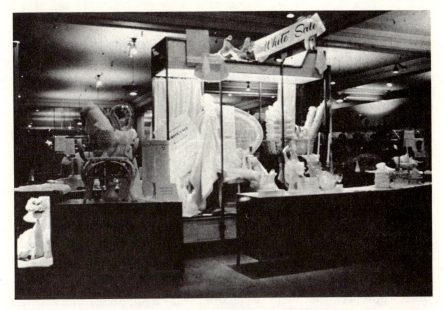

Clearances and promotions can be handled in many ways, such as the semi-annual White Sale. B. Altman's, N.Y., created this handsome setting at the entrance to the linens department for one of their White Sales. (Courtesy of Fairchild Visuals)

Clerks can work up enthusiasm for new merchandise without worrying about pushing leftover stock.

MAKING SALES TIMELY

The customers' finances at time of sale will ultimately determine if it is a success or not. If sales are held immediately after Christmas and at back-to-school time, many families will be without cash. It may be preferable to wait until budgets again are solvent —or offer extremely liberal credit stimulants.

ABANDON ''NO CHARGE'' POLICY

"No charge" policies during sales are being abandoned by many retailers, who realize that not all customers can take advantage of the good bargains due to lack of cash at the time.

CATCHY NAMES

Catchy names are still important. The simple "clearance sale" tag doesn't arouse much interest any more unless bargains are really fantastic. Depending on the season and occasion, numerous names can be used, like "Scratch and Dent"—"Nicks and Knocks"—"Cat and Dog"—"Odds and Ends"—"Wounded, Battered, and Bent"—"S.O.S. (Scratched, Old, and Soiled)."

"Clean Sweep" and "Once In A Season" are also good themes.

Liven up the event by having personal attire and store-wide decor tie in. Dusting caps, long aprons, janitor outfits, and similar attire can be used for "clean sweep" promotions. Feature brooms at discounted prices as a leader item.

"BUTCHER" PRICES

Dress clerks in white jackets and jaunty butcher caps and let them "butcher" the prices. One store used a supply of chickens as a drawing card. These were given with purchases of stipulated amounts. You could tie in with a local butcher and let customers pick their poultry up there.

AUCTIONS

People have a natural impulse to bid, bargain, and barter. Use this inclination to pep up clearance sales. The excitement of bidding may find customers paying higher prices for the merchandise than in a typical clearance sale.

MAKE YOUR OWN DEAL

Advertise that no reasonable deal will be turned down, and then let customers make their own deals. Provide scratch pads and pencils for them to jot down the items, and then let them dicker.

WHITE ELEPHANT

The name itself permits cute advertising and promotional gimmicks. Let customers submit written bids on white-elephant merchandise over a period of several days. On the last day, the highest bidder is called and told to pick up his white elephant. Publish lists of

Auctions are a good way to clear out leftover stock. Make it a community event with stores and residents contributing merchandise.

the successful bidders, with items bought and prices paid to spark interest in future events. Or hold a traditional white-elephant auction sale, in which the items are sold immediately to the highest bidder.

FLEA MARKET

These have become so successful with clubs and private promoters that merchants are taking note and giving them a retail twist. Set up displays and sell clearance items in a flea-market atmosphere in the store, or, if weather permits, outside.

SIDEWALK SALES EVENTS

These continue as good clearance-sale vehicles. See chapter 14 for ideas on how to dress up the typical sidewalk sale.

WAREHOUSE EVENTS

An informal type of clearance sale which really packs them in if the prices and setting are right. Stage it right in the warehouse. Make no bones about it—the event is designed to move merchandise. The very atmosphere of the setting denotes low prices.

LEMONS

Every store has these. Be honest about it: advertise that they have turned sour and you want to get rid of them. Lemon-flavored cookies and candy, lemonade, and lemon-shaped price tags add color.

DRAGON'S DEN

Set up a special area and decorate it as a dragon's den. Netting, webbing, gauze-like materials will give a spidery effect; stone wallpaper will add realism. Splashing water and other eerie sounds can be piped in.

Keep personnel from the room. Install a patio bell to be rung if assistance is needed. Sale merchandise is stocked in the den area; customers fend for themselves. Advertise that life is not always a bowl of cherries; that if customers want true bargains they will have to enter the dragon's den to get them. The very nature of the event will attract.

ATTICS

These carry the connotation of something good being tucked away, waiting to be discovered. Use an upper floor; design it to resemble an attic; dress help in smocks, dusting caps, and aprons; and let them sweep up profits by moving leftovers.

FIRE SALES

Misfortune happens. When it does, a clearance is inevitable. The event can be dressed up with cute "smoked herring" or "smoked ham" labels, advertising that customers have bought smoked ham and herring before, but that they probably have never tasted smoked (fashions, shoes, appliances), and at such low prices, too.

Served smoked items in sandwiches or as hors d'oeuvres.

CASH IN ON GIFT CERTIFICATES WHILE OUT OF BUSINESS

One store which burned down prior to Christmas advertised that customers could still give their favorite gifts by purchasing gift certificates for redemption when the store re-opened in spanking new quarters.

AUCTION BUCKS

Print up a batch of auction money and, for several days or weeks preceding the event, give it with all purchases; or use it as an incentive to get shoppers into the store early, giving it to the first 50 or 100 customers each day, or to those buying specific items.

The "auction bucks" are used on auction (clearance) day, when the store puts the sale merchandise up for sale. Only those possessing auction bucks can bid. Frequently a 50-cent item will go for many dollars in auction bucks, adding to the fun.

LIMITED-TIME CLEARANCES

Clearance sales can be completed in very short periods of time if prices are drastically reduced and the event held when shopping is convenient, such as during evening hours. Merchandise is moved quickly; costs of staging a clearance sale are reduced; the event is over soon and not spread over several days.

Set specific hours, limiting the event to four or five hours. Have drawings to stimulate interest, with a grand prize offered. This pulls because the winner will receive the item within just a few hours, or less, of the time he registered.

Generate added interest by giving prizes each hour. These can be clearance merchandise, with the customer choosing his prize up to a specified amount.

Or put a time limit on and let the winner keep everything he can grab and hang onto within a specified period of time—like five minutes.

Or, perhaps, give him as much as he can gather in his shopping cart in that amount of time.

THIRTEENTH MONTH

This is a new twist to the old inventory sale. It is held during the last week of the year or the first week of the New Year. Retailers advertise they intend to do a month's selling in a few days. Use 13 as the figure around which prices are based. Black cats, ladders, four-leaf clovers, and other superstitious symbols can be used in decor and ads, as prizes, and in contests.

BOSS IS AWAY

While the boss is off on a buying trip, enjoying a sunny vacation, or just home with a headache thinking about all the stuff he has to clear out, the slaves at the store stage a tremendous sale. Use photos of the slaves readying for the clearance; a picture of the boss leaving for his buying trip, off sunning himself, or at home with the ice bag.

LET THE WOMEN TAKE OVER

Run a clearance by letting employee wives get into the act, serving coffee and home-baked buns, and running the store. Female personnel, who will be more familiar with the operation, can be promoted to "boss" to supervise wives of management and owners.

BRING A FRIEND

Frequently it may be feasible to sell two items for the price of one. This is an old gimmick which still pulls. Or sell the second item for a penny or some other ridiculously low price. Give this a new twist and tell customers to bring a friend, suggesting that if one person cannot use two of the same items, he can share their cost with his friend.

COLORED-TAG DAYS

Tie red tags on sale merchandise. When a purchase is made, the customer keeps the tag, which he presents to a local theater for free admission.

Or simply put bright-colored tags on all merchandise to be sold at special prices, thereby designating it as the sale goods.

You might work this on a discount basis, leaving regular price tags on the merchandise but adding colored tags, with each color indicating a rate of discount; e.g., yellow, five percent, red, ten percent.

NOVELTY AUCTION

To the first 50 adults entering the store on mornings (or other specified slow periods) prior to the clearance, give $10 worth of store money. In addition, throughout a stipulated number of days preceding the auction, each purchase entitles customers to a matching amount of store money.

When auction day arrives, articles are put up for sale and only those with store money may bid.

CHAPTER
14

Making the Most of
Outdoor Activtiy

Sidewalk sales continue to draw buyers, and the trend shows every sign of increasing as the great outdoors becomes the password for the relaxed informal younger generation.

Although sidewalk sales are usually held on a group basis, there is no reason why the individual retailer shouldn't do outdoor selling or use the outdoors as much as possible in his promotional efforts. Many of the gimmicks in this book lend themselves well to outdoor use and can be successful with a few minor adaptations.

Tourist areas especially should cater to outdoor activity.

Although June, July, and August were popular months, back in the days when a single outdoor sidewalk event was the only outdoor activity of the year, outdoor selling can now extend into spring and fall. Weekends lend themselves well to outdoor sales.

Remember the children in these events, as they are often responsible for drawing parents.

The best method for handling the display of merchandise is to permit each retailer to use the space in front of his shop. The main street can be blocked off for entertainment and pedestrian traffic (arrange beforehand with city officials).

Non-retail groups should be invited to participate; clubs and organizations will be quick to set up fund-raising activities, adding color and attracting their membership and friends to the event.

Spark outdoor selling with these ideas and themes.

Retailers can make use of sidewalk space. Simple outdoor displays like this can push seasonal items during the year.

START WITH A PARADE

Encourage children to participate; offer prizes.

STROLLING ENTERTAINERS

Throughout the event have strolling bands, guitar players, clowns, merchants or customers dressed in offbeat costumes (award prizes if customers participate); the mayor riding through the area on a mule distributing candy to children. These will add color and generate interest.

CHILDREN'S ACTIVITIES

Provide assorted activities for children, like free or low-cost rides on small merry-go-rounds; pony-cart rides; perhaps a small play area where they can be amused while parents shop nearby.

Simple stunts like this, having a garden tractor pulling a car, are good for a parade. Inexpensive, they would get a laugh in a big city or in a small rural community such as this.

SNACKS

Sprinkle these throughout the retail area, operated by private enterprise, with restaurants joining in, or have area clubs, especially youth groups, operate them.

Ideas include: popcorn venders; ice-cream freezers from which packaged ice-cream novelties can be sold; cotton-candy machines; hot-dog and hamburger stands; soda-pop venders (sell soda in paper cups, eliminating glass breakage); bake sales with emphasis on snack items which can be eaten during the event; various stores can demonstrate outdoor cooking devices, giving samples; set aside an area for an ice-cream social; arrange with a tavern in the area to serve 5¢ beers and free pretzels to customers of age.

ENTERTAINMENT

Displays of old cars, coins, local arts and crafts, and so on can be used; local car and boat dealers can spread out in the street area; a stage can be erected for talent shows, concerts, and other performances; square dances can be staged, using either records or a live caller.

GIVEAWAYS

Giveaways should flourish, with each store using novelty or advertising items like pencils, yo-yos, tops, balloons, and other carnival items with which the kids and adults can have fun. Offer giant-sized shopping bags to make carrying packages easy.

START EARLY

Begin the activity with an early-bird breakfast—free—to those who begin shopping early.

END WITH AN AUCTION

Vow that no merchandise will be returned to the shops when the event is over. Use an auction to get rid of every last item.

FIRST-AID BOOTHS

A must—accidents always happen during this kind of activity.

Themes

ISLAND AND ORIENTAL

Divide the outdoor area into marketplaces; have each retailer dress one up to resemble Nassau, Hawaii, etc.; offer island imports for sale—obtain money from the islands to exchange for dollars; serve and sell food associated with the islands; use thatched roofs, tropical palms, netting, sea shells, bongo drums, voodoo dolls in decor, offering these for sale later in the day if they aren't to be used again. Oriental lanterns can be used for lighting; coconuts make good snack items, also prizes.

Play island music over a PA system. Attire clerks in tropical or oriental costumes; set up a tea room where pineapple juice is served in pineapple shells; serve tropical fruit punches at tea tables. Orchids and other tropical flowers are good giveaway items. Let local artists and collectors display items from the islands. Give ricksha rides to the children. Ask oriental women in the community to conduct gourmet workshops showing residents how to concoct simple island dishes. Have a travel agency participate.

NOSTALGIC THEMES

The old days, be they the roaring 'twenties, pioneer days, Gold Rush days, centennial days, days of the old West, are always good.

Ideas include a "Wild West" or other old-time parade, with prizes to best entries; have a special children's category; give prizes to women dressed in the best old-fashioned costumes. Clerks all are attired from the period emphasized; men can grow beards before-hand with prizes for the longest, best shaped, most original. Use barrels and kegs from which to sell; set up covered wagons and sell like the peddlerman did; hold a square dance in the street; let "prospectors" shovel through a sawdust pile for buried treasure; offer prizes for old coins entered by customers; have an old-time sheriff and deputy add interest by arresting shoppers for nonsensical reasons; hang up salamis and cheese and let customers say where they should be cut; have guess-the-weight contests—if the customer guesses an item's weight right, he receives the item free; serve crackers and cheese, or cookies, from the barrel; put barrels or large crocks of snack items around and let customers help themselves; highly polished antique spittoons are good for serving wrapped candies to the kiddies; have old-fashioned rockers, wicker chairs, benches, milking stools available in front of each store so customers can relax; serve free lemonade or punch, calling it "old firewater."

Tie in with a period of the community history; invite residents and area clubs to help provide props and displays for the event.

COFFEE HOUSES

Set up a coffee shop—an espresso parlor. Go hippie. Invite the area kids to participate—lead the way—show you how.

Advertisements and sales talks should be in their jargon; clerks should dress mod. High school and college students can be hired to

Outdoor restaurants are always fun. Gimbel's, N.Y., set up this outdoor cafe to tie in with a special store promotion. (Courtesy of Fairchild Visuals)

read poetry, display their arts and crafts; give them a soap box and let them make speeches. Decorate with peace and ecology signs and themes. Give the entire promotion a young-generation theme; use rock bands for impromptu performances.

VENETIAN DAYS

Sell merchandise from gondolas; play Italian music; use Italian or water themes in decor; dress clerks in typical attire. If near water, end with a Venetian Day parade, urging all area boat owners to join in. Or move the entire promotion to the water's edge, with all stores selling there.

ARABIAN NIGHTS

Convert counters into bazaars; provide 1,001 bargains; have clerks attired in Arabian costumes; provide Arabian intrigue in contests and innovative gimmicks.

MARK TWAIN DAY

Parades; contests for the best dressed Mark Twain, Huck Finn, Tom Sawyer, Becky Thatcher can be held; Pick a pre-school Tom

Sawyer and Becky Thatcher to reign; stage fence-whitewashing, frog-jumping, watermelon-eating, and other contests. Or conduct a search for the child with the most freckles or warts. Include the local theater, ask the owner to show a Huck Finn movie, with retailers providing free tickets. Prior to the event give out "Huck Bucks" with purchases; on day of the event children can use them for snack or ride purchases. Bamboo fishing poles and corncob pipes are good give-away or leader items.

SHOWBOAT

Store displays resemble a showboat; build a landing pier effect along the sidewalk, with platforms to resemble decks from which merchandise is sold; a lounge or snack area can be in the "Dixie Queen" decor; have outdoor cafés featuring southern hospitality and good food; play Stephen Foster melodies; female clerks dress in Scarlett O'Hara costumes; ask the local theater to show "Gone With The Wind" or another appropriate movies; conduct a Southern "Belle" contest and pick a queen.

Outdoor furniture can be attractively displayed in its natural setting. This tent at Bloomingdale's, Paramus, N.J., is set up 10 weeks a year. It is adjacent to the permanent furniture unit. (Courtesy of Fairchild Visuals)

FANTASY LAND

Selling stands resemble a fairy land. There can be a "Never Never Land" circus, with children bringing their pets; dress clerks in Peter Pan costume and use Peter Pan or fantasy innovations in decor, contests, and theme. There can be train rides for children.

COWBOYS AND INDIANS

Sell from the "Old Medicine Man's Wagon;" set up Indian teepees for real bargains; stage a "Wild West" parade; give away Indian headdresses, hatchets, knives (rubber), and peace pipe for children; serve a "Sheriff's Posse" breakfast for early shoppers or at a snack counter; hold Indian wrestling matches; ask a theater owner to show an old Gene Autrey or Roy Rogers movie; ask area Indians to use the event to hold an annual powwow, selling their crafts and putting on exhibitions and displays.

Tent Events

Like wildfire, tent events are spreading, gaining momentum, and it is unlikely they will burn out. Real tents can be used; or rent an auditorium, an armory, a warehouse, a field, or an oversized parking lot . . . anything that will permit a large gathering of customers.

These can be staged by individual retailers, renting a tent; or by a group of retailers with each taking space in the tent as well as assigned space outside around the tent.

A circus effect can be used with a tent sale. Retailers can work with a promotional firm to bring in rides and attractions, even a midway. Or retailers and area groups can provide their own, with dunking booths, ring tossing, and similar attractions easily worked up by service and youth groups, which can use them to make money. You might even bring a real circus in and let them put on a show; but the area must be big enough so that stores can have space to sell, too.

If the retail group designs its own circus, a lively performance can be offered by hiring skydivers, motorcycle daredevils, and others stunters, who are usually available for one-day or short stands. Bring in a giant-sized roller coaster for the main attraction; perhaps an area farmer has ponies to give children rides in a small ring.

Turn Main Street into a carnival to attract shoppers. Coordinate this "in-store" carnival activity with sidewalk sales and the event can really pull.

Set up number wheels, with tickets given to shoppers as they make purchases. If they spin the wheel and its number matches theirs, they win. Weight-guessing booths, ring tossing, fishing ponds are all easily set up locally.

If it is a local effort, no admission will probably be charged. If a circus is brought in and admission is charged, retailers can absorb all or a portion of it by giving chits away during a specified period earlier to customers making purchases.

Perhaps a rodeo should be considered in place of a circus. Use professionals or amateurs available from a local riding or 4-H horse club. Newspaper ads can be bordered in rope; clerks can wear western attire; customers' contests on the western themes can bt held. A western-styled parade could open or close the event.

GET ACQUAINTED

Use an outdoor sale to let the residents of the community get acquainted with each other. In addition to outdoor selling, entertainment can include mixer-type games and contests (check with city recreation or school or extension-service youth agents for leads on good mixer activities). Children's contests can include sack races, greased-pole climbs, hula-hoop twirls. Adults and even teen-agers can use a square dance to get acquainted. Have plenty of tables around which people can sit and visit.

ONE-NIGHT CARNIVAL SALE

Design around an outside carnival atmosphere. This event is to pull traffic for a limited time, perhaps one evening. Eliminate costly and time-consuming background materials, substituting loud-speakers and carnival atmosphere—balloons, barkers, clowns who mingle with guests. The gimmick is the low prices for the one-night stand.

OUTDOOR COOKING SCHOOL

The outdoors is ideal for cooking schools, especially if emphasis is on barbecues or outdoor entertaining. Turn the event into a garden or patio party.

Groups of stores can go together for this one. If it is a joint promotion, furniture stores can emphasize outdoor and casual furnishings; apparel shops zero in on sportswear, with a short fashion show while the meal is served; supermarkets can provide food and a short discussion on food preparation—perhaps a briefing on newest items in the outdoor cooking line; suppliers may be able to provide demonstrators to handle the actual "school" part of the promotion.

SPORTING EVENTS

Attract men—lads—even women with sporting events or work-shops about sports, in the outdoors. A buffet supper can be served. Bring in a pro and let him give tips; conduct classes over a period of time and then hold a tournament complete with trophies; try things, like archery, in which the entire family can become involved and which can be done at home.

Research what clubs and teams are available in the area and sponsor contests among them; or use members of these to conduct classes and give exhibitions.

MOONRISE EVENT

Everything occult, even witchcraft, can go here; or perhaps you might use a space-age angle.

Shoppers receive tickets during a specified period beforehand when making purchases. These are good for admittance to the event, which includes outdoor shopping under the stars; a small area for a moonlight dance. Supplement the stars with a little artificial lighting if needed.

FIFTY-STATE FAIR

Promote the USA by holding a 50-state fair, with each retailer using a state for background, advertising, promotion, and related sales gimmicks. Highlight products of the 50 states, major industries, culture.

SAFETY CLASSES

These lend themselves well to summer sales events, and can be staged over a 15- to 30-minute period by resource people in the downtown area. Include clinics in boat safety, surfing, skin diving, camping, golfing, flying—whatever is popular in the area. Use local resource people to conduct the event, staging impromptu classes whenever a crowd builds up.

Or go all out: build a portable tank and hold boating or canoe safety classes on the water.

CHAPTER
15

Catering to the Kiddie Crowd

No one can deny that children keep the retail cycle going around. Every time a baby is born, a new customer arrives on the scene.

Some merchants have even learned they can promote for baby before his birth as well as after.

Babies

SHOWER PARTIES

Introduce new baby items with a shower party, inviting all mothers-to-be and new mothers to the event. Have demonstrations; experts from local colleges or extension services can be used to conduct classes and seminars.

Have a well-versed clerk on hand to show new baby merchandise and explain features.

GUESS THE DATE

Expectant mothers register at the store, guessing the exact time their baby will arrive. Each month a review is made, and the best guess wins the title of "New Mother of the Month" and a baby gift.

CLINICS

Baby clinics for expectant parents can be offered by stores as a promotional gimmick. Frequently there is enough local talent

Children are always amused by zoos. Stores can utilize this gimmick during any type of promotion. Alexanders, Paramus, N.J., put birds in its greenhouse to attract the children and then sell plants to the parents. (Courtesy of Fairchild Visuals)

Some stores offer babysitting services and recreational activities for the kids, leaving Mom free to shop. Sandboxes are inexpensive for the stores to maintain and the kids love them. (Courtesy of Fairchild Visuals)

Kiddie rides provide something for the children to look forward to on Mother's shopping trips. The rides should be supervised and they can be run by the store for good will or be a leased operation that charges a small fee for the rides. (Courtesy of Fairchild Visuals)

Pony wagon rides will lure youngsters to area events or keep them entertained while parents shop. The store could put its name on the cart.

Oversize animals cast in plaster or cement are another way of amusing youngsters while parents shop. Locate them in an open area so there will be enough room for youngsters to play without interfering with shoppers.

available from colleges, extension services, hospitals, medical associations, insurance agencies, and civil-defense offices to staff a clinic with classes on a number of subjects over a period of weeks.

GIFT FOR BABY—AND/OR MOM

Some stores may want to send congratulatory gifts to each baby born in local hospitals. Or send a token gift to the mother while she is still there.

Check with hospitals first to make certain the baby lived—too many mail-order firms are sending gifts to all babies reported in newspaper listings, with the result that many mothers receive gifts for a child that didn't live. Local stores can't afford to make that blunder.

NEW YEAR'S BABY

This is still one of the more popular promotions, receiving pages of publicity in almost every community annually.

Most important is establishment of rules beforehand: decide whether the contest is limited to births in a particular hospital or group of hospitals as well as boundaries within which parents must reside. Although this event is usually done on a group basis, with all participating stores contributing a gift, there is no reason why a single retailer cannot go it alone.

One Texas retailer did this, and he has become a legend in his home town, anxiously waiting by the phone, with special lines connecting him to area hospitals. He sponsors radio and TV coverage that begins an hour before midnight and keeps the audience alerted for his announcement. When it comes, he rushes to the hospital to photograph mother and baby, and the picture is immediately flashed to TV viewers.

Prior to New Year's Eve, ads should list what will be given. The contest opens immediately after midnight on New Year's Eve and frequently it's close—with babies born just minutes apart.

BABY-SITTING CLINICS

Customers will especially appreciate baby-sitting clinics. Arrange with schools, extension personnel, or an area nurse to conduct the clinic, giving certificates to those who finish. Lists of qualified baby-sitters can be made available to new mothers by the retail group.

The lists can also be distributed to other families in the community who may need sitters, so advertise their existence and publicize the baby-sitting clinic.

Pre-School and Young Children

COLORING CONTESTS

These are always good; they can include kids from pre-schoolers up. Award prizes by age groups if a wide age spread is used. Handle in a number of ways: print a picture or series of pictures in ads, or let the child draw his own. Pictures are deposited in boxes in the store: Local artists or teachers can judge. When promoting for children is needed, holidays and other occasions like back-to-school time, lend themselves to coloring contests.

BACK-TO-SCHOOL SAFETY PROMOTION

Give a new twist to back-to-school days by working with schools and police officials to make the community safety conscious. Let children submit pictures; display them in store windows. Sponsor classroom visits by area resources people to discuss all types of safety in the classroom. Most schools will be happy to have these added programs.

ART EXHIBITS FOR SMALL FRY

Take the coloring contest a step further and let the small fry have a cultural exhibit; stage a show just for them, featuring their creations; award ribbons and give prizes; display winning entries in store windows; add variety by permitting arts and crafts as entries too. Sculpture, ceramics, model building, and other hobbies qualify by today's standards.

QUICK DRAW CLUB

Shooting contests for children are good, especially if they stress safety and an expert is used to conduct them. Use toy pistols with rubber darts.

Or hold a series of contests using the "pistols," bows and arrows, darts, and other games of skill. Award diplomas for attendance or completion; a prize for high points. Hold events on a regular basis; form teams to have matches. Invite parents and friends to watch from the sidelines.

PHYSICAL FITNESS

Make it a karate or judo promotion. Instructors can be found in most communities now; only a small amount of space is needed, along with a few floor mats. Or get the kids hooked on relaxing via yoga at an early age.

REPORT CARDS

Numerous promotions can be built around these. But be careful. Too much emphasis can be put on report cards, with the result that under-achievers feel they aren't up to par—that they have no chance at all. Everyone can participate if moms become teachers and fill out the "cards," grading the child weekly for his good behavior. At the end of the month the child gets a token gift when he comes in with mother.

RADIO AND TV CHILDREN'S PROGRAMS

These offer a host of new ideas, and retailers can tie in at the kiddie level, not only by sponsoring programs but by participating, too. Check with radio and TV personalities to see what novel gimmicks they can work out.

BIRTHDAY CLUB

Every child likes a birthday party. Start a birthday club and let children register name, address, and age. On the child's birthday he receives a greeting and coupon for a gift, which he can pick up when he visits the store accompanied by a parent.

CANDY

Always a good giveaway whether it's a lollipop from an in-store lollipop tree or old-fashioned candy from a barrel. All children visiting the store should be treated; for sanitary reasons, use individually wrapped candies. If possible, choose candy that isn't sticky or of chocolate (many children are allergic).

Or hold an old fashioned taffy-pull and let everyone get sticky, with the store providing wet paper towels for quick clean-up.

CONTESTS

All sorts of toys from Yo-Yos to model airplanes lend themselves to contests. Try a kite-flying event, with a physical-education teacher hired to give kids tips on a Saturday morning on the store's parking lot while parents shop.

SPELLING BEES

This intrigues youngsters, and many can be lured to spelling bees. Hold on Saturdays, while parents shop, employing a teacher to conduct the event. Give these novel twists by sometimes quizzing on history, math, geography, and related items.

BALLOONS

Helium-filled balloons, with tags attached so finders can return the tags for a prizes, are good novelties for children. The tags are numbered, with store keeping a master list. The child lists his name and address on the tag on the balloon and also on the master list. He lets the balloon go; the tag returned from the farthest away means a gift for the child who released it. The person returning the tag might be given something, too.

POINTS FOR SALES

Post a large wall chart on which each child's name is recorded. As parents and friends make purchases, they indicate which child receives credit for the purchase. Each week the amounts of purchases are added and posted. At the end of the month the winner receives a prize.

CHILDREN'S DAY

Take advantage of the annual holiday or choose your own time to honor area children.

Include a parade, with prizes for the best homemade costumes; provide a game area on parking lot or by sealing off a spot in the retail area where games and contests can be held; crown a king and queen (bathing-suit contest for girls and life-guard contest for boys). Games can include sawdust-pile scrambles for pennies, potato-sack races, apple bobbing, greased-pole climbing.

PET GIVEAWAYS

These continue to build enthusiasm with young shoppers, but they also meet with parental and humane-group resistance, with mistreatment and neglect reported. If pets are given, a stipulation should be made in the rules necessitating parental approval of the prize. Better yet, give a stuffed animal for a gift, with the live animal turned over to a local zoo. If live animals are used, add interest by giving unusual animals like a Mexican burro or a goat.

If the child is to receive a live animal prize, give a book of instructions on proper care; possibly include a cage, food, and other needed equipment.

ZOOS

Rent animals for display in store windows during children's events. Or the retail group can set up a small zoo to interest children while parents shop. If animals are used in stores, eliminate unsanitary conditions by laying canvas on the floor and covering with thick layers of wood chips.

ANIMAL SHOWS

Local equestrian groups can stage pony or horse shows on store parking lots; or you can hold turtle races, frog-jumping contests, even a pet show, with every child bringing his own pet.

FISHING PONDS

Borrow this from the country fair and install a large "pond," in which gifts are placed. Children fish with poles until they hook a package, which they keep.

Or work through a commercial promotional firm which uses real ponds, with real fish. Children keep the trout they catch.

PHOTOGRAPHS

Still gaining in popularity are photograph sessions at retail stores wherein babies and children's photographs can be obtained free or at low cost on certain days. Commercial firms which do nothing but this type of work are usually used, but there is no reason why a local photographer can't do this job.

Contests built around baby or child photographs will also spur interest. Baby-of-the-month events are good. Post photographs of all babies photographed during the event and have an impartial judge select the winner. Obtain permission from parents to use the photo in store ads. You could do this once yearly and name the child the store's official baby; give him a gift and have him present during events.

Or photograph all children brought into the store during a given period; post their numbered pictures (without name) on a bulletin board; have an impartial person judge; and name a winner.

Give little egos a real boost by making window space or a bulletin board available on which children can tack snapshots. For many tots this is the only public attention they will ever receive. If placed in the window, the pictures will draw considerable interest from sidewalk shoppers.

TALENT CONTESTS

These are good for children over six. If possible, arrange for the winner to appear on a local TV program. The show can be held in the store, on a parking lot, or outside in the street if a retail group event.

Or arrange for the show itself to be a TV program at the local station.

Regardless of the mechanics of staging the show, the gimmick is to use the winning act, or several of the top acts, in in-store promotions. Have them make guest appearances during events or stage impromptu visits to the store. The latter is good if singing happens to be the talent.

SPECIAL WEEK

Take advantage of special weeks throughout the year to work in child-oriented community activities. During Fire Prevention Week, arrangements can be made with firemen to give all school children a ride on the fire trucks. Not only does this acquaint them with firemen, but it gives teachers an opportunity to stress fire-safety procedures while interest is peaked. Retailers can provide hats, badges, and other items to the little firemen.

Other "weeks" during the year also lend themselves well to such activity.

SCHOOL TOURS

Encourage teachers to bring students into the retail area for class tours. Arrange special hours (during slow periods) when clerks can take time out to meet with little folks, explaining how the store operates. Let them try the cash register, ticketing merchandise, etc. Give demonstrations on products in which small children are especially interested.

KIDDIE CREDIT

Not really so ridiculous. Many stories have opened charge accounts for kiddies, with parental approval, limiting the amount which can be charged and arranging for small weekly payments. This teaches the child all about credit at an early age, and he learns to meet his obligations.

PARTICIPATE IN COMMUNITY PROGRAMS GEARED TOWARD CHILDREN

Frequently children and their community activities are forgotten by busy retailers. Most Scouts, 4-H'ers, church and school groups welcome retail help and support.

Ideas on how retailers can participate abound in every community; as an example, in one mid-Michigan community retailers participate in the annual 4-H livestock fair. They bid on animals, purchase them, and receive a certificate for in-store display.

This can be carried even further. The animal can be donated to a children's home or orphanage or to a needy family; or the store can throw a barbecue, inviting customers to taste the fine products raised by local youth.

Retailers can also stage shows, make store and window space available for project display.

KIDDIE PARKS

These can be established either in stores or outside in the retail area on a large or small basis. The main thing is to gather together some items on which children can play while parents shop. If a central park is established, then someone should be hired to supervise it so children don't wander off and get lost.

GO-CART RACES

These are good, and frequently the retail district is the only place where enough paved roadway is available for them.

RECORD HOPS

Pre-teens are getting into the act on this once teen-age activity. Add interest by staging one, either with disc jockey or with live performers, for the younger members of the community.

STORE MASCOT

Acquire an unusual animal and make him the store mascot; let the kiddies name him; use him in ads and promotional efforts; encourage children to stop and visit him.

COMPACT DISPLAYS

Make shopping easy for children by small, compact displays which stock their favorite items.

KIDDIE PARADES

These can be held alone or as part of a larger parade. Let kiddies join in, "doing their thing" however they like. Or make it a "Wheels Parade," with children having to ride bikes, wagons, scooters, or anything with wheels. Encourage them to use costumes by giving prizes for the most unusual.

CHAPTER
16

Winning Over the Youth Market

Teen-agers continue to be a group unto themselves. Not only do they like to be considered independent, but most of them are to a great degree.

They like to shop on their own—and they shop in stores which cater to their needs.

The emergence of stores, often operated by teen-agers or persons in their early twenties, in recent years, emphasizes this vast market had not been served in the right way. Not only are these youth-owned stores successful, but they are selling merchandise which is definitely good quality, style setting, frequently in the higher price ranges. Often the items are hand crafted, even by young people themselves.

The trend will apparently continue. Recent statistics say that by 1975 about 60 percent of our estimated 235 million population will be in the 18 to 34 age bracket.

Retailers who have lost their teen market, or who feel it slipping, will do well to visit a typical teen-type "Beads and Bangles" operation.

Creating the Right Atmosphere Is Important

No longer do mere signs like "Teen Center" suffice in building a teen-age department.

Low lighting; colorful decor (which speaks in the teen vernac-

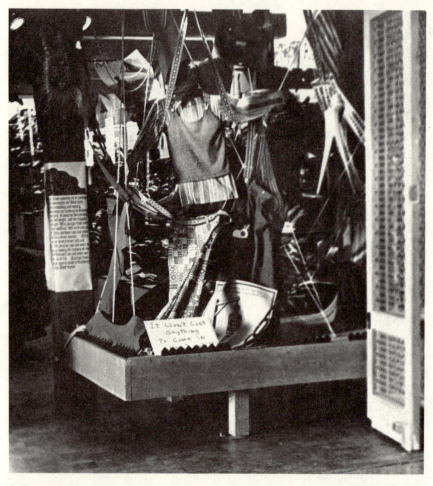

Informal displays in their own area of the store will attract teen shoppers. The current fashion look is a must, and the displays should be kept simple and uncluttered.

ular); the sweet smell of incense or candles burning; and displays that indicate a "with-it-ness" are needed.

Fad items continue to be the rage. But teens don't go for mass marketing. They like to have their beads-and-bangles just a little bit different, so keep inventory high, diversification great. No more "several gross of a kind" stocking of novelty items, but rather an admixture of many designs and styles will add to the overall atmosphere.

GIVE THEM A PAD

Teens need and demand a place where they can meet, sit down and relax, and rap with friends before making the big decision.

Give them a place, maybe a coke bar—anything with an informal setting, even if it's just a few bean- or air-filled plastic chairs or some oversized pillows on a huge throw rug on which to sit while discussing their purchase.

RESERVED SALES PERSONNEL

Personnel should remain reserved, available only when called on, unless they have a unique relationship with teens and are accepted by them. Generally, today's teens are independent—at the most interested only in what their peers approve of and often not even caring about that—but definitely not too concerned over a saleslady's opinion.

Pushiness doesn't work with them.

BUY FROM TEENS

Many retailers are finding that specialty items made by teens are instant sellers. These can range from novel works of art, pottery, craft, or jewelry items to quality, well-sewn attire.

Teen-Age Life Styles

There definitely are several subcultures in the teen-age group. One is the teen still in school; another the dropout teen, who also has his own group; and then the older teen—the person who is too old to be part of the school-teen crowd, yet too young to be accepted by the adult community.

Most stores or departments catering to teens will be serving all three subcultures, so it is important to be aware of their existence.

If only the school group is catered to, a large number will be eliminated. Frequently the older teen group is the leader group, to which the other two look for guidance. Although they may not participate actively in school-oriented activities, they are still very much a part of the crowd. The dropout students also have some influence, and if neglected completely by retailers they'll find shops elsewhere which cater to their needs. When the word has spread, younger (often school-aged) teens will follow. Better to make all feel welcome, promoting not only for school teens but for the vast group on occasion.

School-Related Gimmicks

There will be times when retailers will find it necessary to promote around school events. Sometimes these promotions may have to be limited to students only—but at other times all teens can be invited to participate. Gimmicks which have a definite school tie-in and which can be used for that age group only include:

SPONSOR SCHOOL PROGRAMS

Participate in school events, helping with fund-raising activities. Use school colors in store windows and displays. Donate cards for school programs with store name imprinted on them. Give the schools a gift like a scoreboard or a trophy case.

SENIORS' DAY

Set aside a day near graduation and turn the city over to seniors. They can work in stores, offices, public facilities. Retail gimmicks include giving a percentage of the day's sales over to the seniors for a graduation party or trip.

Or host a party for them that evening.

If all retailers can't be enticed to participate, a store or a few stores can stage this alone, teaching seniors stock control, merchandise marking, how customers are served, office procedure.

Seniors wear name tags so they are easily recognized; clerks are named their hosts and give them personalized assistance; perhaps even take them to lunch.

TEEN CONSULTANTS

Many stores use teen consultants obtained from among the teen-agers themselves. Either hold a promotion with interested teens competing for the positions, or work through schools using teens in the retail classes. The consultants help store management decide on buying; give advice on what merchandise teens want in price ranges, colors, and styles. Store policies affecting teens can also be developed from this group.

CAREER DAYS

Every high school has a program centered on helping students plan careers. Retailers can get into the act, developing a retail-oriented phase with teachers and consultants.

STUDENT EMPLOYEES

Co-op programs are a reality in many schools, with students working half days in stores and obtaining high school credit. Stores can co-operate with schools by hiring students to make the program successful. Retailers can also be valuable resource people, helping make the program successful and updating techniques.

YOUTH EMPLOYMENT CLEARING HOUSE

Set up a youth employment clearing house. Students and non-students can leave name and address, other personal data. Stores can use this when in need of part-time employees.

HELP THOSE WHO DROPPED OUT

Work with local school administrators. Obtain lists of drop-out students or publicize that dropouts needn't be "left-outs." Get industry and businessmen together, along with professional members of the community. Hold classes in retail and in other related business and professional areas. Help train the youths and place them in various jobs: stockrooms, shipping, billing, sales. Perhaps a co-operative learning situation can also be provided where they can learn some of the social manners which are often lacking among this group but necessary if they are to be self-supporting. (No preaching—put someone who speaks their language in charge).

If possible, arrange half-day work sessions, permitting them to earn money yet enabling them to attend school either part time or by correspondence. Or arrange for night classes.

By taking an interest in this subculture, retailers can eliminate one of their nuisance problems: students who hang around in front of stores or who make themselves conspicuous because they feel a lack of attention. Provide the attention and eliminate the nuisance.

INCLUDE THE HANDICAPPED

Many communities have handicapped students who desperately need money and, more important, the feeling of being accepted, wanted, needed, and part of the group.

Find job situations where these students could be used and then seek them out, using school and ministerial members of the community to find them.

LUNCH-INS

Work with school officials to stage a lunch-in, with business-men having lunch with various groups in the school cafeteria. The retail group can pick up the tab for the day. This may be the way to get across messages to teens on programs planned for them or on problems which have arisen in which teens play a role. Given a chance, teen can be helpful.

What better way to discuss shoplifting and similar problems than by throwing a lunch-in, with retailers and police officials rapping with students. But be careful—don't turn the students into guilty culprits. Make the pitch educational, not preachy. Give them the true facts—how much merchandise is taken yearly; what the legal and criminal consequences can be; and how they and other customers must absorb the loss in cost of purchases.

If done several times during the year, make certain that not all programs are geared toward helping the retailer: throw a lunch or two just to entertain the kids—to get to know them, to close some of the generation gap.

TRADING STAMP-IN

Frequently students will want a large item for their school but can't afford it. Stores offering the same type of trading stamp can assist by arranging for the purchase with a specified number of stamps. Students will generate sales by their very enthusiasm and will help plan promotions to aid the project.

Window displays that are built around "youth" themes lure teens into the store. (Courtesy of Fairchild Visuals)

SCHOLARSHIPS

These are always good. Why not a retail-oriented scholarship from the retail group?

WINDOW DRESSING

Today's students are among the most creative ever. They are full of good decorating ideas. Use them to come up with ideas for windows or to actually dress windows. They can also be used to help in store decor, especially for their own departments.

RESOURCE MATERIALS

Stores can supply a host of materials to schools for teacher-aid use. A math teacher regularly visits hardware stores in his community to obtain a supply of fall sales circulars. He uses these instead of texts to teach percentages. Store display materials can be used in retail classes. Other brochures, selling aids, and retail materials might well be adapted to social studies, business, and other classroom use.

An annual or bi-annual meeting between retailers and teachers can develop educational programs in local schools incorporating retail-provided aids. Students are more stimulated when they recognize firms involved in problems or discussions they are working on.

Promotional Activities for All Teens

SPECIAL CLASSES

Even though many teens are no longer students, they are interested in learning, and subjects can range from beauty and hostess courses to car customizing.

No segregation is needed—boys pay a lot of attention to their hair (how about a session just for them?) and many girls would find a "powder-puff" auto-mechanics course helpful. Drug seminars are exceedingly popular (especially if former addicts are used).

Check with teens; find out what they are interested in and what classes, workshops, or seminars they would like in a non-school atmosphere.

"RAP" SESSIONS

Have younger members of the retail community, or those that think young, get out and talk with the kids. Find out what they want; what their concerns are; what projects they are vitally interested in; how the two groups can work together to help each other and the community. From these, retailers can quickly learn what teens feel is lacking in the retail community.

FESTIVAL

What was once referred to as a street dance has now become a block party or a festival. The music is faster and up a few decibels, but basically the rest of the program is the same. Invite teens to participate but don't be surprised if there's little dancing—teens often like to listen to concerts by live groups, and may prefer to stretch out on the lawn or floor instead of dancing or sitting.

Charge no admission, or keep it low. Keep stores open so parents and others can observe. This can do much to promote goodwill and greater understanding between the oldsters and the long-hairs.

BATTLE OF THE BANDS

These are also well liked, but most teens never experience one due to lack of facilities. Hold in a retail area or parking lot, using a makeshift stage and an ample supply of electricity, and the promotion is underway. Let bands register beforehand, each one performing for a stipulated period of time. Add interest by erecting two stages, opposite each other, so that one group can be setting up while another is playing. This insures continuous music, keeps the crowd interested, and prevents early dispersing and milling around.

When it's over, the crowd decides winner. Or name a panel of judges from the crowd to pick the winner.

The winning band gets a monetary prize—the rest get token payments, usually just enough to cover expenses.

MARATHON—THEY SHOOT HORSES, DON'T THEY?

Bring back the roaring 'twenties—the movie has already created interest and paved the way. A Roaring 'Twenties party, based around a dance marathon (the theme of "They Shoot Horses, Don't They?"), will keep teens busy. Invite parents to watch—but not participate.

Or make it an all-age event, pitting teens against adults to see who lasts longer; encourage all kinds of dances and give prizes.

INFORMAL FESTIVAL

These spontaneous things can go a long way to show teens that retailers care. On specific nights make an area available to them. Let the kids bring guitars and have their own little festival, sing-a-long, or whatever appeals. No organization is needed here—just provide the room, it can be informal: just a place where they can sit or sprawl out, inside or out, and they will take it from there.

TEEN CENTERS

Retailers really wanting to cater to teens can create a teen center, or be active in having community groups work together to form one. Round ice-cream tables or huge old oak tables and chairs will do. Tiffany-type lamps, pop art panels, mod wallpaper, and an assortment of old furniture repainted in bright enamel and coupled with modern plastic air-filled forms will do.

If retail oriented, the center may be used only as a place to congregate after school—or open it evenings and weekends.

EMPLOYMENT SERVICE

Finding teen employment is more of a problem than most adults think. Rules and restrictions governing child labor make it almost impossible for kids to obtain jobs. Most make the rounds many times to no avail. Yet they are constantly berated for being shiftless and lazy.

The retail group can be a leader in forming an employment service to handle teen employment for all elements of the community. Use a publicity program so residents and others can phone their needs in, even if it's just a grass-cutting or gardening job.

TEEN FAIRS

These can include a multitude of ideas, and the manner in which they are staged is limited only by the community facilities. Include in these the things teens are interested in; style shows; new auto showings, especially of sports cars; educational and career exhibits; arts and crafts demonstrations; hobby demonstrations; young hostess courses with the accent on home entertaining; demonstrations by home economists on table-top cooking and making oddities like Hawaiian food; instructions on how to throw a party, how to throw a shower.

The fair could include youth tournaments of sports like archery, golf, and other items not normally offered in school. Let all students participate.

If many stores go together and the facility is large enough, a fair similar to the Home, Sports, and Auto Shows many retail groups sponsor for adults can emerge for the teens.

Wandering bands, or guitar strummers, can mingle among spectators. Use contests, prizes, and games to add color.

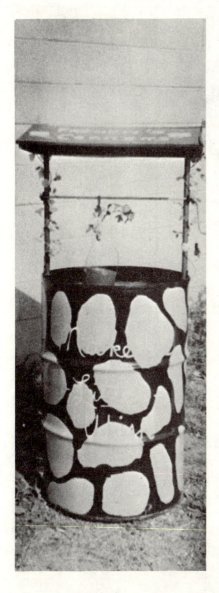

Contests involving teen clubs can be used to inspire such worthwhile community projects as providing trash cans for area roadside parks—even for spots in the retail area. Publicity and prizes will spur interest. Retailers can supply the barrels, teens supply the paint and imagination.

Comic strip, television and radio characters are popular with the "youth market." They can be used effectively in displaying merchandise that appeals to the "youth market." (Courtesy of Fairchild Visuals)

DISC JOCKEYS

These resource people are still popular. Teens know and respect them. Live broadcasting from the event itself is sometimes possible, permitting teens to get into the act, talking with the disc jockey.

ECOLOGY

Gimmicks with an ecology twist will attract teens. Even youths who aren't too concerned about other community problems respond to appeals for river cleanups, bottle collections, paper drives.

The retail area is usually the only location with enough space available where cleaned-up materials can be stored. It is also a central point, easily reached by most.

Offer stores or warehouses for drop-off points; get in on big cleanup programs, hosting the kids after the job is completed and publicizing their efforts by using pictures in store ads, saluting them for a job well done.

USING MIXERS ON EXCHANGE DAY

Odd as it may seem, there are many teens who are shy and retiring. On Exchange Day they stop in at the store, meet other students, enjoy a coke, and watch demonstrations. Keep it low key, using mixers to get the kids acquainted. Cut prices on a few items to put them in the buying mood.

TREASURE HUNT

Add a touch of mystery to a sales promotion by hiding things and giving clues. For instance, a series of pictures could be used, with animals hiding in the scene as are used in small children's magazines; or hide an object, like a lipstick used as a bottle stopper. Cute little rhymes, giving hints, can be used to add intrigue and help them find the hidden object.

JUNIOR MISS PAGEANT

Have your own beauty pageant, picking a Junior Miss to represent the store or retail group. Enough contests are sponsored to provide ideas on how it can be done. Gimmicks also include holding modeling, make-up, poise, grooming, and other workshops beforehand for girls interested in competing. The stores should work closely with the local junior high and high schools on the beauty pageants. The workshops on grooming, poise, etc., may be part of hygiene class or physical education class, for example, good posture, how to walk properly and exercise necessary to keep fit—all in preparation for the pageant. The clothing stores participating should have the girls model their clothes in the pageants.

YOUTH COORDINATOR

Stores, or retail groups, can hire a youth coordinator whose sole job is to work with youth in a host of public-relations projects. Just introduce her to the kids, via ads and visits to schools. If the coordinator is adept at working with them, the kids will take it from there . . . she won't be able to keep them out of her office. (Or make it a he—boys may shy away from a female coordinator, but both boys and girls will be intrigued by a male, especially if he is young.)

ROOMMATE EXCHANGE

This is designed to serve teens living in the community while attending college. Install a bulletin board in the store where they can post notices when they've lost a roommate. Landlords catering to students can also use the board.

Make Teens Welcome

This is perhaps the most vital gimmick of all in luring teens as customers. MAKE THEM FEEL WELCOME.

Frequently retailers actually discourage teen shoppers. By their very actions (watching them like hawks because they are suspicious all teens are shoplifters or potential rioters), some retailers actually force teens from the business district.

Complaint of teens congregating in front of stores only makes matters worse. Set up a center—invite them in. Go out and rap with them; make an honest effort to talk and not just to criticize. Respect their right to their style preferences just as you expect others to respect your right to yours.

Treat teens with respect and you will get respect in return. Give them a chance. But, most of all, make them feel welcome in the retail district.

They may be teens today—but they are tomorrow's adult customers.

CHAPTER
17

Here Comes the Bride

Even the traditional wedding is changing, with less formality oftentimes placed on the once-solemn occasion.

Recent years have seen weddings held in the most unorthodox manners (at least this is the feeling of the old-fashioned traditionalist): underwater with bride and groom skin divers accompanied by a skin-diving clergyman; in a field surrounded by nature with the emphasis on simplicity; in an old mill; on horseback (these were riding enthusiasts); in the depths of a mine (with the tourist-minded mine owner paying costs for couples wed in the mine); and even as a feature of a nightly talk show on TV.

This isn't to say that the traditional wedding and all that it entails is on the decline. It isn't.

But there can be no denying that many new demensions have been added to the wedding scene. Progressive retailers should keep abreast of these, adapt their products and services to the needs of today's bride—unusual though they may be.

FASHION SHOWS

The bridal fashion show continues to be popular. Make it a real event, including mothers and even fiancés. Some stores hold these on semi-annual basis, having a bridal showing or tea in February for spring brides and an August one for fall and winter brides.

Local bakeries can exhibit wedding cakes to be cut and served later.

Florists can show their lines; don't forget those who sell imitation flowers, which many brides now prefer.

Travel agencies can also be included.

Stage it alone, or turn it into a community affair, possibly using an auditorium. Or hold the event on TV for added glamour.

Invite engaged couples and their attendants to be guests, with a spectator section provided.

NEWSPAPER SHOPPING TOURS

These are ideal ways for groups of merchants to emphasize the bridal season. A special supplement is used, featuring articles on weddings ranging from etiquette to "who-pays-for-what" information. These are merely fillers, with the main feature a running commentary on the bridal tour a local engaged couple made through the retail district. Each store participating receives one photo, showing store manager or clerk with his bridal product or services and the couple.

Each store presents a gift to the couple as payment for the right to use their pictures in the supplement.

The mass effect of this promotes the community as an adequate place for all bridal needs.

BRIDE OF THE WEEK

This is especially good for shops catering only to brides. Each week a bride who purchased her needs from the store is picked from those who have been married during the previous week. Use her picture in store ads.

BRIDE OF THE YEAR

All those planning weddings during the coming year are eligible to enter the contest. The store year runs from June 1 to May 31. Participating stores offer gifts to the new bride. She is outfitted from head to toe and given items for her home if hardware and furniture stores are included.

GARDEN PARTIES

All brides like these. Florists and bakeries can join in, also travel agencies. Use a park-like setting outside to stage the event, inviting the bride and female attendants. The community-type garden party could be staged on a parking lot, if need be, by using fake grass, buckets of plastic trees, Japanese lanterns, etc. Have a brightly colored tent available in case of rain—or advertise a rain date.

The garden party can include demonstrations and hints on everything from planning a garden shower to a live fashion show featuring bridal attire.

REMEMBER THE GROOM

The groom is a necessary part of every wedding, yet retailers have frequently forgotten him.

Fashion showings should include attire for the groom and his attendants. Ideas include loungewear, attire for the honeymoon. Shows featuring hardware and household items with which the groom will soon become acquainted can be held in conjunction with other stores.

Or throw a shower for the groom, giving demonstrations on how to do simple things around the house, offering gifts, etc.

Bridal Register

Not only are these popular for individual stores catering to brides, but for entire community groups which include jewelry, hardware, discount, and furniture stores and others with which the bride will be involved.

Although each store or group of stores will handle bridal registration in the manner best suited to its needs, there are some elements which are important and can be included for both individual store or retail-group effort. Among ideas are:

SELECTION OF PATTERNS

This is important, especially for china, silver, crystal, table linen. Don't forget items like furnishings—nothing worse than receiving a mod lamp to fit into an Early American home.

Keep a list of items which have been purchased for each bride. Another list may include items she specifically wants, along with their prices, so customers can use it for quick reference. Have the bride choose a number of items in a wide price range so all customer needs can be served.

CONSULTANTS

Stores catering to brides and offering register services may find consultants necessary, if all needs are to be filled. These employees will have no other duty than to keep abreast of the retail scene, acquaint themselves with new products, trends, styles, and tastes. The field is really specialized; but this is one service brides will really appreciate.

KEEP STOCK PLENTIFUL

Keep inventory high, especially on items and patterns which brides have selected. Disappointment will be widespread if numerous customers want to give the bride a specific item only to find that what she selected is not in stock. Close checks between regitration lists, inventory, and buying is needed.

OFFER VARIETY THROUGH BROCHURES

Many brides will want something different. Even if the store is unable to sell many novel items or patterns, consultants should have a wide variety of sales brochures and folders available from which brides seeking the unusual can make selections to be ordered.

PHONE AND MAIL ORDERS

Stores serving as registrants for bridal gifts can offer mail and phone shopping. This is one reason brides like to have their preference registered. It means they will receive useful and desired gifts, and shopping by their guests will be made easy.

DELIVERY

Gone are the days when guests brought bulky gifts with them to the church or reception. Gifts are now delivered to the home of the bride prior to the wedding, with many preferring the store deliver the gift so they don't have to intrude on the family while it is making wedding preparations.

GIFT WRAPPING

A must; elaborate wraps are especially desired.

COMPLETE BRIDAL SERVICES

Some stores have bridal departments, complete with consultants, which handle the entire wedding. Included are rental of the white church carpet; ordering of invitations (some even offer hand addressing of envelopes and mailing); reception arrangements, including dinner, buffet, and site rental; flowers; cars and drivers; photography; music both at church and reception; and going-away plans, including pre-planned trips in conjunction with travel agencies.

COMMUNITY BRIDAL SERVICES

Smaller stores which cannot afford this service but want to provide it can group together. Include a bridal shop; a men's wear store which rents formal attire; a florist; a jeweler; china, crystal, and silverware shops; a small department store; a photographer; and several restaurants or hotels equipped to handle receptions.

The retail group can jointly hire a consultant who familiarizes herself continuously with the various stores, products, and services the participating members have.

PERIODIC CHECKS WITH BRIDE

Even shops which are geared toward sophisticated registration will find they cannot control or monopolize bridal gifts. Many friends will shop their favorite stores regardless of where the bride has registered; and this is their right. They will obtain pattern information from those close to the bride and then go out and buy.

This means that bridal lists kept by the registrar may not be entirely accurate at all times. Prevent duplication by periodic checks with the bride to learn what items have been received from other sources and record these at the store.

MULTI-STORE REGISTRATION

If the retail group is based in a small community or organized on a community bridal registration basis, the above registration problems will also arise.

Persons buying gifts which are obviously wedding presents can be asked who the bride is. At the end of the day each store reports purchases, including mundane items like ironing boards and bath towels, to the central registration office. This could be a retail-group headquarters or simply a person who volunteers to take on the job. Then, if a shopper indicates she is having trouble deciding on a gift, the store owner can call the central registration service to learn if a similar gift has already been purchased.

Word of community services like this can be quickly spread by joint advertising when it is begun; by mentioning it in ads later, and to brides and to customers buying gifts.

CHAPTER
18

For Men and Women Only

Plain adult men and women shoppers like to be remembered, too. Make a special effort once in a while to cater to each, or both, of them.

Ideas can include:

Him

REMEMBER THE FORGOTTEN MAN

That can be the theme. Invite men down some evening; tell them you haven't forgotten them. Order in special merchandise just for them, using special in-store and window displays. Hold contests, entertainment, demonstrations; provide snacks and perhaps cute clerks dressed in special costumes. Give the men "stewardess" type treatment and make it a night they will remember.

IN-STORE COMPETITION

Spice up everyday sales with novel contest ideas like installing a basketball net and giving men five tries. For every basket each one makes, he receives a percentage off on his purchase.

WORKSHOPS AND COURSES FOR MEN

Just as women and teens like workshops and instructional courses along with their retail sales promotions, so do men. These

A clearly designated sporting goods shop, such as this golf shop, will attract more than your quota of men. (Courtesy of Fairchild Visuals)

can range from single one-shot deals featuring grooming, dieting, weight control, and wardrobe planning, to things like woodworking, refinishing furniture, minor auto repairs, etc., depending on the type of store.

Hold these in the evening or on Saturday mornings; keep them informal; and the men will turn out.

Her

WOMAN'S DAY

Make it a "Woman's Day at (Store Name)," and initiate a buying spree by crediting purchases made by each woman with points for her favorite club. The points are later converted to money, and the funds used by the groups for their projects. Luncheons, shows, teas, etc., can add glamour.

MANUFACTURER TRUNK SHOWINGS

Many women like these as they have a unique opportunity to obtain items not normally sold.

HOMEMAKER DAY

Salute the homemakers in the community. Tie in with beauty shops offering a discount, and restaurants offering a noon luncheon special; provide play areas for tiny tots. Lower prices on homemaking articles, and give demonstrations designed to make homemaking easier or more glamorous.

PACKAGING PROMOTION

One women's shop feels that any time a woman buys an item for herself she is buying herself a gift. They pack it nicely, wrap it, and put on a bow to make her feel it's something special.

FORUMS

Women today, especially homemakers, like to be informed. Forums on diet, child nutrition, family health, and similar topics lend themselves well to a series of short forums.

All women like to keep in shape. Holding exercise classes at the store is one way that Macy's, Rego Park, N.Y., attracts many potential shoppers. (Courtesy of Fairchild Visuals)

CHAPTER
19

All You Need to Know About Contests

Contests continue to be popular, not only among national firms, which advertise theirs in national magazines and newspapers, but also at the local level.

Many persons have taken to entering contests as a hobby.

Although retailers won't stage contests on the grand scale that manufacturers do, retailers can stage small-scale events either alone or as part of a bigger promotion.

Among items which should be considered before going into a contest are:

1. When it will begin and end.
2. Who will judge.
3. When judging will take place.
4. On what basis winner will be determined.
5. Whether or not the contest will have a special theme.
6. What contestants must do to enter.
7. Whether to use official entry blanks or just plain paper.
8. Whether a qualifier, such as proof of purchase, is necessary for entry.
9. Whether there will be restrictions regarding such things as age, sex, residence.
10. What will be given as a prize.
11. How ties will be broken.
12. Whether entry blanks must be deposited in the store or sent in.

Holding a contest in the sporting goods department can increase sales, in addition to creating a lot of good will. (Courtesy of Fairchild Publications)

13. Where entry blanks can be obtained.
14. Whether prizes will be limited to one per family.
15. Whether there will be a limit to the number of entries an individual may submit.
16. Whether employees of the store will be disqualified, along with families of judges, store management, advertisers.
17. Whether the contest conforms to state statutes (if your state has gambling or contest statutes).

Judging

Judging should be on impartial basis; seek qualified judges from outside the area in the field in which the contest is held. Judges' decisions should be considered final; no attempt should be made by store personnel to discuss the contest or entrants with judges beforehand.

Themes

There are many themes around which contests can be worked, and many have been included in previous chapters in this book. So we won't elaborate on special holiday or business tie-in events.

The following ideas are in addition to others already listed and are primarily contests for contests' sake or generalized ideas which can be fitted into holiday or other events with minor adaptations.

CHECKERS CONTEST

Hold a continuous game of checkers, or have several tables going at the same time. Award a prize to the winner of the most games.

Other games can be used; tournaments might evolve.

DO-IT-YOURSELF PROJECTS

Stores catering to do-it-yourselfers can hold monthly contests exhibiting the work of customers and awarding prizes.

MELT THE ICE

Install a large cake of ice in the store and have a swimsuit-clad model sit on top of it on a cushion. Customers guess how long it will take to melt it.

Or freeze a fish inside a cake of ice and give two prizes: one for the person guessing the weight of the fish and the other for guessing how long it takes the ice to thaw.

LIVING EXPENSES FOR A YEAR

A year's free living is still a popular prize in contests, which can range from jingles to essays or actual physical participation events.

Payments should be advertised first; and these are paid as established, regardless of how much the winner's actual expenses are. Estimate the expenses on the basis of what would be considered normal life in the community involved. Include rent, groceries (perhaps for a family of four), car payments, spending money, electricity, gas, water, entertainment, barber and beauty shops, laundry, lawn mowing, snow removal, heat, baby sitting, telephone.

SPONTANEOUS CONTESTS

Have spontaneous contests which will keep customers from checking the item out. For example: announce over the store PA that a certain tree in the mall area is the subject of a height-guessing contest. Customers are invited to drop their guesses into a box, with the event to end in a half hour and winner announced. Items like this draw interest, give customers something to go home and talk about; they require little promotion and need no advance publicity or advertising. Mention them in later ads so readers will know what they are missing and begin shopping the store to get in on the action.

Or set a definite date on which your spontaneous contests will be held to spur up slow-day activity.

MAKING USE OF LOCAL HAPPENINGS

These always lend themselves well to contests, and making predictions is an easy way to use them: when a strike will end; how many gallons of water are used per day; how many cars pass a certain corner every 24-hour period.

FROZEN RIVER

Any city that has a river can hold a contest to determine either when it will freeze completely over or thaw. To determine freezing, a floatable object is placed in the river as it begins icing up. When the object stops moving, the river is frozen. For thawing, the object must work free from the ice and sweep past a pre-set marker.

GUESS THE VALUE

Display an assortment of merchandise in the window; customers guess what total retail value is; winner takes all.

PRODUCT-ORIENTED CONTESTS

Customers guess certain features about your product lines. Have them guess number of tufts in a 6'x4' rug; the number of shoes in the stockroom; how many of a certain item the store has in inventory.

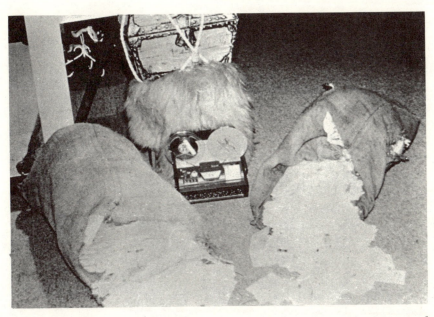

Displaying contestant responses can stimulate interest in your contest and attract more entrants before the final drawing. First prize in this contest was a mink coat. (Courtesy of Fairchild Visuals)

GUESS WEIGHT

Clerks can guess weight of customers; or have customers guess the combined weight of the store's sales force.

LIARS' CONTEST

Although organized annually on a national level, this can also be promoted on a community-wide or retail-store level. Have entrants submit their lies about anything or establish a certain topic. This is especially good for hunting, fishing, and sporting events.

MATCH FIRM AND PRODUCT

Get people interested in the community. At a certain time give out papers with two lists: firms on one side, products on the other. Customers in the store at the time contest is held must match the right firm to the right product.

CHAPTER

20

Tailoring Your Gimmicks for the Shopping Center

Now a vital element in most communities, shopping centers have introduced many new dimensions and aspects to retailing.

Compact—yet loose—they sprawl out, offering a multitude of stores under one roof. Novel architectural arrangements make them attractions in themselves. Well designed, they contain an assortment of facilities for staging elaborate group promotions and for serving as a community facility. Frequently desirable items lacking in the CBD can be found in a well-designed shopping center. Expansive parking lots, well lit and landscaped, are attractive. So are the store hours, designed to serve everyone regardless of his working schedule.

Unlike in the CBD, where retailers are loosely knit and with a history of divisiveness, occupants of shopping centers often seem more unified. Frequently they participate in center promotions which include planned activity for all.

Generally, all gimmicks suggested in other chapters can be utilized by retailers in shopping centers too. Many of those suggested in the chapter on the CBD and retail unity can be converted for shopping center use with a little adaptation. They are designed for group activity.

Other ideas which retailers in shopping centers might find appealing are:

Directories will tell shoppers where they are in the shopping center and where everything else is located. Note the numbered signs on the directory indicating which parking lots are located outside of specific stores. Have numerous directories throughout the shopping center for customers' convenience.

SPECIAL NEWSPAPER SUPPLEMENTS

Promotional ventures of the center can carry more impact if the newspaper advertising is done in a single "center supplement." If scheduled activity is to take place, list it for easy readability. Such supplements may be kept by readers while the rest of the paper is thrown away.

LIST ALL STORES

Frequently only major stores in centers become well known. From time to time lists of all firms in the center can be published.

INTER-STORE REFERRALS

One of the attractions of shopping centers is the variety of

FOR MAIL ORDER — SEND THIS ENTIRE PAGE

Description

Store Name	Page No.	Quantity	Item Number	Size — Color — (Second Choice)	Price Each	Total

Allow at least 3 weeks for delivery

Please, No C.O.D. orders

Shipping Charges to be billed _____

Add 4% Mich. Sales Tax _____

TOTAL _____

STORE HOURS: STARTING NOVEMBER 27 THRU DECEMBER 23 - MONDAY THRU FRIDAY 9:30-9 P.M., SATURDAY 9:30-5:30

Abercrombie & Fitch • **Apogee** • **Ask Mr. Foster Travel Serv.** • **Bally of Switzerland**
Barricini Candies • **Bernard Wig Salon** • **Bonwit Teller** • **Capper & Capper**
Colony Interiors • **Continental Exclusives** • **Crown House of Gifts**
B. Dalton, Bookseller • **Danby's Store for Men** • **Faber's Fabrics** • **Gulian's**
Mackenzie-Bostock-Monroe • **McBryde's Boot Shop** • **McSweeney's Foot Wear**
The Marilyn Shoppe • **Mark Cross** • **I. Miller Salon** • **The Mulberry Bush**
Nino of Somerset • **Optical Fashions** • **Page Boy Maternity** • **Claire Pearone**
Furs by Robert • **Saks Fifth Avenue** • **Schettler's Drugs** • **Schrafft's Restaurant**
F. A. O. Schwarz—Toys • **Sherman Shoes** • **Standard Federal Savings**
Don Thomas Sporthaus • **Walton Pierce** • **Charles W. Warren**

MAIL ORDER TO: SOMERSET MALL GIFT GUIDE
2801 SOMERSET MALL
TROY, MICHIGAN 48084

CHARGE TO: ☐ My Store Acct. ☐ BankAmericard ☐ Master Charge
☐ Amer. Express ☐ Security Charge ☐ Diner's Club

CHECK STORE AD FOR CHARGES ACCEPTED BY EACH STORE

CHARGE ACCOUNT NUMBER _____

☐ Check or money order enclosed
please no cash

NAME _____

☐ Send me your Christmas Catalog

ADDRESS _____

☐ Put me on your mailing list

CITY _____ STATE _____

☐ I'd like to open a charge account

ZIP CODE _____

PHONE NUMBER Area Code ( ) _____

15

Shopping centers can use joint mail order forms for shop-at-home customers. A good special promotion or holiday gimmick—many stores can use one brochure. Note the vast selection of charge accounts listed.

stores involved. If one doesn't have an item, another probably will, eliminating need to drive elsewhere.

This benefit is lost, however, if the customer isn't helped in his search. Not only should clerks in each store know what all departments stock, but they should be familiar with various cate-

Shopping centers can house community recreation centers. This covered-mall shopping center turned the plaza into an ice skating rink. (Courtesy of Alan Hicks Photography)

gories of merchandise available in other stores. Periodic tours of the center by clerks will acquaint them.

Or print a directory listing merchandise by category, with names of stores handling the items listed. These reference lists should be available to clerks—possibly even to customers.

FULL FAMILY SHOPPING CENTER

Housewives don't shop alone anymore. Frequently the entire family makes an afternoon or evening of it, especially when at a center. Restaurants, snack bars, and vending machines are important elements. Facilities should also amuse small fry, and these can range from in-store benches to mall-area group activity.

TRANSPORTATION CENTERS

The vast expanses of land on which shopping centers are located lend themselves to development of transportation centers to serve

Parking lots can be used in more than one way. Turn the lot into a carnival with rides to amuse young shoppers and provide a recreational area.

customers arriving via many modes. One developer projects assorted transportation needs in his plans, providing helicopter pads, commuter railroads, local buses, and vast parking lots.

DISC JOCKEYS WILL LIVEN THINGS UP

Shopping center malls are prime locations for disc jockeys and live broadcasts. Let them interview and chat with customers as they walk across the mall.

MALL DISPLAYS

Keep activity going in the mall area to make it seem lively.

Professional acts may be used; or bring in local groups for displays, demonstrations, or entertainment. Art exhibits, photographic exhibits, contests, hobby displays, arts and crafts classes, judo and karate exhibitions or classes; displays of community equipment like

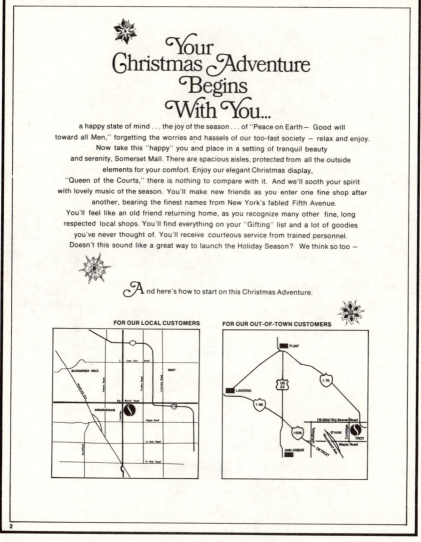

Shopping centers, generally located in the suburbs, can use maps in joint or individual store ads to show customers the way. Keep such maps simple—the less clutter the better.

a new or original fire truck; new automobile showings; 4-H, Scout, and other youth activities; service club displays and membership recruiting booths; school groups and their related activities; women's club activities with things like flower shows, Christmas recipe swaps; political "meet the candidate" outings or booths.

Shopping centers can gain the good will of the community by making mall areas available to local groups, such as a scout troop or charity, for fund-raising projects. Provide display counters and advertise their presence on shopping center bulletin boards and directories.

The possibility is endless. Anything that is going on in the community may lend itself to mall display or demonstration. The sources are no farther away than the local newspaper.

FASHION SHOWS AND DEMONSTRATIONS BY
PARTICIPATING STORES

Stores in the center complex can utilize mall space from time
to time with their own showings and demonstrations, which will
be traffic stoppers.

COURTESY CENTERS—LOUNGE AREAS

Install areas where shoppers can meet, have a cigarette, refreshment. Rest rooms can include plenty of mirror and vanity space.
Phones, car rental services, drop boxes for utility bills are all gimmicks which can be located in the mall area for customer convenience.

SLOGANS, CARTOON CHARACTERS, SONGS

One slogan, character, or song can represent the entire center,
aid in unifying merchants and in emphasizing the development.
Involve customers in helping to pick these—maybe even write them
or draw them.

COMMUNITY ROOMS

Use is unlimited—for retail classes sponsored by the center or
tied in with local schools; in workshops for residents; clubs; in-store
training sessions; mass meetings of store heads.
If available to the public, emphasize this.

DISCOVERY CENTERS

In early 1970 an educational magazine announced "discovery
centers," describing them glowingly as ". . . educational facilities
being introduced in to shopping centers in the United States." Designed for pre-schoolers, the areas give children an opportunity to
use their instinctive ability to learn. Mechanical games, fiber glass-
reinforced seating units which double as play structures, and other
educational items were used in supervised areas while parents
shopped.

UNUSUAL ATTRACTIONS

Bring in unusual attractions, like an old English double-decker bus to give customers a quick tour of the outside mall area; a hurdy-gurdy man, an old-fashioned popcorn wagon, balloon artists, marionette shows.

COOPERATION WITH CITY OFFICIALS

Frequently, city officials are under pressure from established CBD merchants who resent shopping centers coming in. This can lead to criticism, which sometimes spreads throughout the community. It may be desirable, especially in developmental stages, to establish goodwill and community relations with municipal officials, cooperating with them in every way to meet local rulings. One center helped the city improve traffic after opposition claimed the center would be a traffic hazard. The center donated 25 feet of its frontage on both sides, valued at $1 million, for widening the road for a fifth lane. It also erected de-acceleration lanes to move traffic off the road into its parking lot without slowing down other traffic.

CHAPTER
21

Luring Tourist Dollars

More jobs, higher income levels, and more customers: these are among the direct results of effective tourist promotion, and any community can achieve it.

Whether a business traveler, a family on vacation, or a youth group, tourist dollars are left in almost every community a stranger passes through.

Example: in 1966 over $1 billion was spent in Michigan by tourists. Over 140,000 jobs were dependent on the tourist trade, and it had become the state's second largest industry. By 1968 tourist spending increased to $1.1 billion and in 1969 to 1.35 billion.

Of prime importance in capturing tourist dollars is attitude. Businessmen must recognize the value of tourist trade if they are to benefit from it.

A number of years ago the U.S. Department of Commerce stated, "If there's a road leading in and out of your community there's a fair chance of attracting tourists."

They pointed out that highways may be helpful, but they aren't a must. While many tourists are attracted by well-developed, sophisticated recreational and pleasure facilities, there are just as many who prefer to poke around in the backwoods.

Primarily, tourists want comfort, change, fun, and friendly surroundings.

Any community that can offer these basics can build a tourist industry. It has been estimated that a few dozen tourists in a city

daily throughout the year is comparable to acquiring a new manufacturing industry.

Money spent by travelers is new money, brought into the
community and it circulates. Unlike that of residents, who have
patterned spending habits, the use of the tourist dollar is more diversified. It reaches hotel and motel owners, operators of recreational
facilities, restaurants, gas stations, and retailers. Even farmers who
supply fresh produce and professional men who write more insurance
on recreational businesses benefit. For them, the dollars pass through
the community, generating business over and over.

But, like most things, tourism doesn't come easily. Competition among communities for tourist dollars is growing keen, and
many are luring tourists with sophisticated campaigns.

Just selling a community on tourism can sometimes be a difficult
job. This is especially true in areas which cling to the "status quo"
philosophy. Of prime importance is group action, with business,
community and civic, service, women's, and professional groups
working together.

This chapter is divided into two sections, each dealing with
gimmicks designed to help gain tourists as follows: luring and attracting tourists, and gimmicks in serving tourists.

Luring Tourists to the Community

TRANSPORTATION SURVEY

Study highways serving the community; survey where present
visitors originate and use those areas as targets for advertising and
promotional efforts. Survey bus, train, and airline services, for their
users are potential customers on which to zero in.

WORK WITH TRAVEL AGENCIES

Make contacts with travel agencies in other areas so they are
aware of your area and can promote it.

COMMUNITY LISTINGS

Make contacts with recreational and travel organizations and
clubs; supply them with literature, and if they have events listings,
get your community included.

SURVEY COMMUNITY ATTRACTIONS

Make a list of area attractions, both natural and man-made, and list them so information on what is available can be used as a starting point. Then develop or encourage private developers to provide complementary attractions, which can range from novel innovations to something as well rooted as development of a community facility now dormant.

BUILD A YEAR-ROUND TOURIST AREA

Early in developmental plans, consider a year-round tourist program. There is no longer such a thing as a dead season. Liven things up in off times. Summer fishing resorts have gained a new breed of guests in winter months by providing heated swimming pools, skating, tobogganing, sledding, old-fashioned horse-and-cutter rides, even skiing as attractions. In between, many communities sandwich in hunting, mushroom and berry picking, wildflower and fall-color tours as lures to visitors during spring and fall, to round out the calendar.

REMOTE AREAS ARE ASSETS

If yours is a completely remote area, capitalize on that—it alone can be an asset.

DINING FACILITIES

Unusual dining spots, even small country inns, have a personality of their own and can draw tourists, especially if they feature gourmet specialties related to the area and not commonly offered.

ETHNIC BACKGROUND

Survey the area's ethnic background and hold an annual celebration highlighting events, customs, costumes along the ethnic theme. Take this a step further and make it a year-around promotional effort, with the community becoming famous for its German, Italian, Chinese, Bavarian, or other ethnic personality. Carry this through in building design in the downtown, in clerks' attire, in sales

Historical themes and festivals are a good tourist lure. Utilize and display any memorabilia, not only during a promotion, but at any time. This display at a shopping center relates to the American Revolution. (Courtesy of Fairchild Visuals)

promotions. Encourage residents to participate and restaurants to serve special dishes.

GO HISTORIC

Build a program around the community's early settlers or go back to the Indian days. If there are descendants of the original Indians still in the area, include them as an integral part of the culture and society. Restore their customs and attire, rebuild early settlements, stage reproductions of early historic events. These things interest travellers.

PROMOTE THE AREA

Launch a progressive advertising program. Most states have tourist or commerce bureaus which promote the entire state. These are frequently broken into sections, and the regional organization

Auto window stickers can be provided by retailers or other business groups to promote the entire community.

is broken into county or similar-sized units. Contact state and regional agencies in order to be included in their programs. These agencies receive numerous requests yearly, and costly brochures and booklets are mailed to those enquiring.

By working on a regional basis, the entire area can be combined to lure people. Once there, smaller communities work for their share of the tourist business. But unless the joint regional effort is made, tourists will look to those areas which offer a wide range of activity. Most tourists do not spend their entire vacation in one small community, even though they may make their base there. Side trips are taken into surrounding areas. So whole areas must work together to lure the tourist to the region.

TOURIST SHOWS

One way to lure tourists to an area is to take booths in sport-, tourist-, or travel-oriented shows. These are in large cities. Example: many Michigan and Wisconsin communities take booths in Cincinnati, Cleveland, Milwaukee, Green Bay, Chicago, and Detroit shows. Southern states are also represented there, as are those from other areas. The reason: these are concentrated areas of mass numbers of potential tourists. Use items from the area to decorate the both; provide an area personality in the theme. Costume people staffing the booth; give away brochures on the area as well as advertising novelties.

GIVE AWAY A VACATION

Gain word-of-mouth advertising by giving away a free vacation. Visitors register at the booth, and at the end of the show a name is drawn. The vacation cost is divided among local businessmen (or paid by the group). If divided, area firms offer coupons or letters indicating what they are giving: restaurants provide meals; gas stations, gas; amusement attractions give free passes; motels and hotels offer lodging.

Capitalize on this when the guests arrive by sending publicity, complete with pictures, to their home-town news media.

Have dignitaries meet them on arrival; name an official host to guide or accompany them if they want someone along, but recognize that many may prefer to scout around alone. Don't forget a rousing send-off, as that will be their last impression. Provide a take-home gift basket with samples of area products.

ENCOURAGE TOURIST BUSINESSES

Encourage operators of tourist attractions to locate in the community just as you would seek new retailers and industry.

PRESERVE AREA HISTORY AND SITES

The historic boom continues with museums, large and small, sophisticated or located in converted barns, lighthouses, old stagecoach stops, old mills, schools, town halls, fire halls, or grocery stores drawing travelers. Every community can preserve its old items in an inexpensive way. A public appeal will bring out an assortment of items. Keep a catalog of item and donor. If enough related items are gathered, specialized displays can be made. Contacts with state historic societies or nearby universities will provide professional advice and help; perhaps even students to get it going.

BE IMAGINATIVE

Communities without special products or items around which to promote can use history in building events. Use something broad and general, like an ice-cream social worked into a weekend festival. One community did this, with an old-fashioned fair approach featuring old and new flavors; an assortment of hand-cranked churns on which residents and tourists pitch in; a sundae-making contest with a year's supply of ice cream as the prize; an ice-cream king and queen; a hearty ice-cream breakfast; an ice-cream-eating contest.

RURAL AREAS ARE GOOD

Rural areas provide a wealth of resource material for tourists. Many farmers are capitalizing on travelers, taking in tourist families. City-raised children enjoy seeing cows milked, participating in haying, gardening, chicken feeding, berry and fruit picking, fishing in farm ponds, walking in woodlots, and other activities enjoyed by country boys years ago.

Entire farms can be developed into tourist resorts, and the area can return to the old-fashioned methods of harvesting to add color. Retail areas can take on the country look, both inside and out. Home-style country meals, with all guests gathered around a common table, add atmosphere in area restaurants. Simple country games like croquet, horseshoes, huge overflowing sandboxes will keep little folks happy.

Areas not rural in nature but which want a rural effect can make an Old MacDonald's Farm-type zoo, using farm animals and letting children feed them.

THE THEATER

Summer theater draws tourists. Every community has its would-be stars. Often all they lack is organization, leadership, and a meeting place. Headquarters can be in a dusty old attic above a store, in a long-forgotten opera house, or even a former barn. Or stage productions out in the open.

USE AREA RESOURCE PEOPLE

If a university is nearby, work with staff and students to develop tourist attractions. They may even survey the area and make recommendations. They offer a supply of energy, imagination, know-how, and helpfulness, and all they need is an invitation.

One community used college students to retrace part of the Lewis and Clark trail in the area. It's now a haven for canoeists, campers, and hikers.

CONSERVATION OFFICIALS HELPFUL

Work with state, federal, and area conservation officials for ideas and suggestions on how to promote the natural aspects of the area.

MOCK ARRESTS

Have local police slow down a car, picked at random, on the highway near the community. Escort the occupants into town, lock them in the hoosegow for picture taking, and then make them the community guests for a day, weekend, or whatever. (But tell them about it when they are "arrested"—maybe the occupants of the first car halted won't be able to spare the time and another will have to be hailed.) Send publicity about their arrest and good time to their local paper.

PROVIDE ENOUGH HOOPLA

Festivals require one thing—hoopla—and lots of it. All tourist events should feature prizes, giveaways, balloons, costumes, product demonstrations, gadgets, contests for young and old, colorful posters and decor, imaginative displays.

COLLEGES ARE ATTRACTIONS

Colleges, like other community facilities (survey those in the area), can be attractions. Many have botanical displays, unusual architecture, planetariums, skating rinks, and other recreational facilities open to the public. They will usually permit tourists and residents to participate and will assist in promotional efforts.

BRING ALONG A CAMERA

Hold contests with prizes for the best pictures taken in the community during a given period or special event. Winning entries are published in the local paper and a copy sent to the winner's home-town paper so publicity can be gained. Install a bulletin board to display photographs.

ON LOCATION

"Anatomy of a Murder" gave Marquette, Michigan, a real boost, tourist and publicity wise, in the '60's. Movies have done the same for countless other communities. Mayor John Lindsay has become as well known as many Hollywood personalities in his endeavors to bring moviedom to New York. He knows this means extra pay checks, extra sales, filled hotel and motel rooms, an influx of tourists, free publicity, and that movie firms often rebuild or build new facilities which can be used by the community when their work is done. In Marquette a tavern used in "Anatomy" was expanded and remodeled, and it is still an attraction drawing tourists.

FLOWER FESTIVALS

Festivals built around flowers are good. Holland, Michigan's tulip festival has won world-wide fame with its colorful hues, authentic windmill brought over from Holland, wooden shoe parade, and celebrations.

LOOK AT WHAT'S HAPPENING TO SIBERIA

Even the Russians have gotten on the tourist bandwagon. Siberia, the long forgotten part of the world, became a new vacation spot early in 1970. Associated Press reported that mysterious Siberia, until now the place of banishment for Russia's political dropouts, was being opened up to summer flights by American tourists. Service between Anchorage and Khalbarovsk was given the Soviet okay. Ten flights were reported booked immediately, including 1,200 persons, from June 6 to September 27. Trips were from 8 to 15 days and included hotel, ground transportation, meals, theater tickets, sightseeing excursions. A 15-day package included a side trip to Moscow. Stewardess uniforms were designed around the glamorous Czarist days, and airline flights featured menus with borscht, caviar, sturgeon, and chicken Kiev.

That is tourist promotion at its best.

INCLUDE THE MILITARY

Even America's military has gone tourist. Many military installations are open to the public (good public relations), and local communities are encouraged to include them in promotional efforts. Some even have unique military displays; mock battles are staged on weekends; military units participate in area parades and events, including aerial maneuvers.

BRING BACK THE RAILROAD

One small midwest community had 17,000 people ride a little railroad train "from no where to no where", and it was advertised as such. The 23.2-mile ride in coaches over 45 years old was the first railroad trip for many. Passengers gleefully tossed and shook their way through a scenic area, pulled by steam engine.

EVEN NONSENSE WILL ATTRACT

Nonsensical nothings will have a long way to go to beat Gaylord, Michigan, where townspeople annually burn their "problems" on Alpenfest Day. Tourists participate, writing problems on bits of paper, which are stuffed into a papier-mâché effigy of a rotund man and burned on the main street. The "world's largest coffee break" is then held.

MEMENTOS

Mementos from an area can be almost anything. At Long Beach, California, one of the huge 35-ton propellers from the retired ocean liner *Queen Mary* was melted down and made into 18 million tie tacks to sell at $1 each. Each will result in word-of-mouth advertising by its owner.

EVEN THE LONDON BRIDGE

Even the London Bridge has gotten into the act, with its purchaser rebuilding the monument at Lake Havasu, Arizona, where it is bound to become a curiosity in desert promotions he has planned.

POTPOURRI

A potpourri of ideas around which tourist attractions can be built include: battlesites, burial grounds, old forts, barracks, settlement buildings, dams, lumbering camps, mines, churches, schools, farms, homes of former settlers famous or infamous, museums of general or specific nature, famous old trees, rocks and other earth formations around which legends can be spun, bridges, lighthouses, local industries, tours of area sites, craft shops, old-fashioned printing shops or blacksmith shops, modern power plants, unusual local crops, botanical gardens, orchards, blossom festivals, parks and preserves, game farms (either domestic or wild), fish hatcheries, old opera houses or movie theaters, old circus grounds or county fairgrounds, beauty pageants.

This book would never end if all the ideas were to be included. Those herein are meant to show diversity and provide a basis from which areas can become tourist meccas.

Also endless is the list of ideas around which communities can build events. Included could be: pirate festivals, fishermen's balls, early morning flapjack breakfasts, ducks or other wildlife-calling contests, ox roasts, hobo conventions, motorcycle hill climbs, skin-diving festivals, plowing and harness-racing contests, fall-color tours, clothesline art shows, potato-picking contests, mule days, ham-and-egg shows with meals judged first and then sold, log rolling, hillbilly days, a waiter's tray race.

Tourist Service Gimmicks

Regardless of natural or man-made attractions, or even the best planned event, SERVICE is a must when catering to tourists. They must be made to feel welcome, not only by retailers but by the entire community. This takes tremendous education if all residents are to be inspired to treat outsiders with courtesy and consideration. Each community can originate its own brand of hospitality, depending on how its tourist program will be developed.

PROMOTE FRIENDLINESS

Smile at strangers; be the first to say, "hello." If strangers appear to need directions, ask if you can help. Urge clerks to do the same.

KNOW THE AREA

Read all Chamber of Commerce brochures; keep them on hand for reference. Never permit a clerk to tell a stranger she doesn't know where something is in the community. The byword should be that, "if one doesn't know, one finds out."

SERVE THE FAMILY

If the area has always provided entertainment primarily for one member of the family, provide activities for other members. Example: the old "cabin up north," where the entire family wilted away while father fished, has long ago fallen by the wayside. New operators have recognized that today's wives aren't going to sit in an inconvenient cabin for a week or two. New facilities now lure the resorters, and they offer recreation halls with games for children. Retailers catering to tourists can learn from this. Provide special shopping days and attractions for wives and children. Give them something to do.

RAINY WEATHER PROMOTIONS

The tourist market is a captive one on rainy days. These guests are just waiting to be lured downtown as outside activity is curtailed. Have a fast promotional plan ready which can be sprung quickly when raindrops fall; use radio spots to advertise it.

REMEMBER TOURISTS AFTER THEY'VE LEFT

One small midwestern retailer built a clientele stretching east to New York, north to Canada, and south to Florida. Customers from ten states send mail orders after they've left. The store is in a small crossroads community, but the owner promotes brand-name sportswear with a real flair. Clerks make friends with all strangers, and each is asked to register. At Christmas each receives a personalized card and note from the owner thanking him for stopping in and inviting him to vacation in the area again next year.

INCLUDE TEENS

Peg activities toward teens and encourage school, church, and teen groups in the community to make special efforts to include vacationing teens in their organized activity.

COME AS YOU ARE

Informality is the way of the vacationer. "Come as you are" signs make them feel welcome.

INCLUDE TOURISTS IN AREA ACTIVITY

Include tourists in area activities as active participants. If there is a parade, ask them to enter or to judge; if tourists return annually, ask them to participate in staging events held while they are there. One community holds a motorboat race annually, and tourists serving as judges or in other capacities receive "commodore" status and take home a framed citation. The gimmick is to frame the citation to insure it will be hung. Folded or rolled ones get tossed into desk drawers and are forgotten.

DON'T DOWNGRADE OTHERS

Know what is going on in surrounding areas and don't downgrade those events to inquiring tourists. This will be spotted for what it is; it ranks in the same category as downgrading a competitor.

SOUVENIRS

Provide souvenir items for sale which are representative of the community, perhaps reproductions of something local. To provide these it may be desirable to give birth to a small local industry, which can also be an attraction.

WELCOME BANNERS

Welcome banners in windows and on light poles make tourists know they are truly welcome. If a special group or convention is in town, print banners including group name.

COURTESY PAPERS

Provide free morning newspapers for each room in area motels. Small stickers attached can say, "Good morning, this paper is courtesy of (store name)."

GIVEAWAYS

Simple, inexpensive, imprinted giveaways for tourists to use when on vacation and then take home are good. Included are plastic rainbonnets for ladies, ball-point pens, nail files, combs. All are items typically left at home but needed.

OVERSIZED SHOPPING BAGS

Shopping bags, imprinted with store and community name, are good. They help with shopping and will be used back home where they will promote the area. The gimmick is to make them strong and attractive.

MYSTERY SHOPPER

To know how the community really looks to a stranger, put a "mystery shopper" into action, but don't publicize it until later. Have him visit hotels, motels, gas stations, and stores asking questions, seeking information to test the knowledge, courtesy, and service of area firms. His report will be revealing for many.

DAILY ACTIVITY LISTING

Let tourists know what is available each day. This can be done in a number of ways: by printing and distributing visitors'

Welcome To The
2nd Annual

PROGRAM

Thursday, Sept. 11

10:00 a.m. to 1 p.m. — Festival Art
    Show Judging — —.O.O.F. Bldg.
    Jerri Hart Show with Charlie Reeder
    WPFB — Festival Center Stage
11:00 a.m. Arrival of Gov. Rhodes — Warren County Air-
    port Press Conference, Golden Lamb
12:00 Noon — Man On The Street Broadcast, WING **Radio**
1:00 p.m. Official Festival Opening andCrowning of
    Honey Festival Queen, at Festival Center **Stage.**
    All Concessions and Booths Open
    WCNW Radio Live Broadcast
6:30 p.m. Radio Control Small Aircraft Demo
    by World Engines, Inc.
    Moon Mullins Show, WPFB, Festival Center
7:30 p.m. Parade
8:30 p.m. Crowning of "Little Miss Honey Bee"
    Festival Center Stage
9:00 p.m. Sweet Adelines — Festival Center **Stage**

Friday, Sept. 12

11:00 a.m. — Concessions and Booths Open
12:00 Noon Man On The Street — WING Radio
2:00 p.m. WCNW Radio Live Broadcast
5:00 p.m. Acrobatic Honeybees — Festival Center **Stage**
6:30 p.m. Paul Steiner Family Singers
    Festival Center Stage
7:30 p.m. Firemen's Parade
8:30 p.m. Stollers Band — Festival Center **Stage**
9:30 p.m. Bayes Band — Festival Center **Stage**

Saturday, Sept. 13

11:00 a.m. — Concessions and Booths Open
12:00 Noon Man On The Street — WING Radio
2:00 p.m. WCNW Radio Live Broadcast
6:30 p.m. Radio Control Small Aircraft Demo
    by World Engines, Inc.
7:30 p.m. Parade
8:30 p.m. Introduction of Festival Queen and
    Announcement of Float Contest Winners
    Festival Center Stage
9:00 p.m. Waynesville Sing-Out, Festival Center **Stage**

Simple listings of all activities such as this one used by the Honey Festival at Lebanon, Ohio, will provide needed information for tourists. To be successful you need cooperative distribution by stores, banks and other business and civic organizations.

guide booklets, which list all activity and which are distributed freely so they are readily available; by providing copies of visitors' guides for all motel and hotel rooms, campgrounds, and other places where tourists lodge; by use of a centrally located community bulletin board to provide last-minute information; by having listings available at a central location for easy pickup with racks in area firms; by sponsoring a daily radio or TV listing of all area activity; by asking pastors to list activities from the pulpit at each service and to include printed sheets in bulletins distributed at services; by having the local paper print a weekly front-page listing of activity.

FILL REQUESTS FOR AREA INFORMATION

Potential tourists will expect, and rightly so, that their requests for information on the area are answered quickly. Brochures can range from simple ones to complete booklets, depending on the resources of the community. The main thing is to provide something.

DETAILED MAPS

Maps of the area should be distributed freely. Those which serve best are those which have a legend and list facilities and attractions.

POSTAL CARDS

Updated cards should always be available for sale in local stores. Provide courtesy ones as a gimmick. These are great for word-of-mouth advertising, and when viewed in that light are an inexpensive form of advertising.

SPORTS TIPS

Areas catering to fishermen, hunters, skin divers, and other sportsmen should give tips daily on areas where these people might be successful. Radio and TV are good media for this. Stores can sponsor the service.

ENCOURAGE LOCAL LEGENDS

Tourists are curious people and will thrive on local legends. Print these and widely distribute them to newcomers in the area.

ADVERTISING FLYERS IN RESORT AREAS

Stores catering to resort areas can print flyers and have them distributed to cottages and resorts. Personal delivery or mailing to an entire area via the boxholder method are ideas.

SPECIAL SERVICES FOR SPECIAL GROUPS

Provide special services for special groups: a flush station for campers; camping sites in area parks; well-marked nature trails are ideas.

EARLY MORNING ADVERTISING

Peg messages toward tourists on radio early in the morning. Many of them are up early to be out for the day. Set aside a specific time each day, and publicize it, when tourist-oriented broadcasts will be transmitted.

INVITE TOURISTS TO PARTICIPATE IN AREA CLUBS

Many tourists are members of service and other clubs and would like to maintain attendance records. Use a signboard to list all area clubs, complete with date, place, and hour of meeting. An invitation for outsiders to feel free to attend will suffice.

CHURCH LISTINGS AND HOSTS

Many tourists include church as a vital part of their vacation. Include church listings in activity schedules. Go a step further and provide listings of hosts by denomination, giving a selection of numbers which out-of-towners can call if they desire to attend services with a local family. Churches will usually participate in these endeavors.

BABY-SITTING REFERRAL

If the community has large scale events, a community-wide baby-sitting service for out-of-town people may be used. Or arrange to have referral lists left in area resorts so sitters can be obtained.

AREA COLORING BOOK

Design a coloring book featuring things in the area for wide distribution to both local and tourist families. This is a public relations device which will promote the area.

CHAPTER

22

Extra Efforts That Pay Off

Among miscellaneous promotional gimmicks are the following, grouped together in categories when possible.

Industrial-Oriented Gimmicks

GIVE BIRTH TO A LOCAL INDUSTRY

Often retailers can be instrumental in helping form a local industry. Listen to customers who have ideas, who are interested in getting started, and refer them to Chambers of Commerce or other officials who can help. If there is a local product not being pushed to capacity, or around which a novel innovation can be worked, retailers can organize a meeting and attempt to form a locally owned and operated corporation.

KNOW YOUR INDUSTRY

Acquaint residents with local industry. Sponsor a series of radio, TV, or newspaper ads around this theme.

INDUSTRY OPEN HOUSES

Set aside a day or week to honor industry, and ask industrialists to cooperate by having open house. Retailers can pick up or share the tab and help provide guide aides for tours and staff for buffet tables.

Local youth groups frequently get involved in clean-up drives and other ecological projects. Retailers can participate by offering refreshments and prizes, but most of all by endorsing and publicizing these events.

During a special promotion, decorative shopping bags are "walking" advertisements. This shopping bag was for Macy's "Far East" all-store promotion. (Courtesy of Fairchild Visuals)

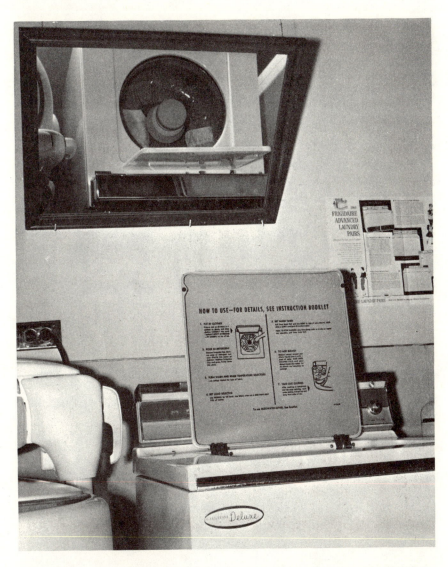

Simple display gimmicks like placing a mirror on a slant above a washer helps a clerk point out the inside of the machine without the customer having to bend over to see inside.

PAY OFF IN $2 BILLS

Emphasize how much area industry means, or how much a specific industry means, in dollars and cents, by having employees paid in $2 bills for one pay period. Seek cooperation of a local

Fashion shows can be built around any type of promotion. This eye-catching backdrop served to set off the newest fashions. The models are carrying simulated mirrors. This was Ward's effect to create a fashion image. (Courtesy of Fairchild Visuals)

banker to get the bills. As these circulate through the community, people become aware of the role industry plays.

PRODUCTS DISPLAY

Local products are placed in store windows along with brochures and signs for each firm, or outside in a mass display. Invite teachers and students to tour.

SERVE ON INDUSTRIAL COMMITTEES

Retailers should be active on local industrial committees, as many leads come their way and these can be passed on. If no committee is active in seeking new industry, retailers can form one. U.S. Chamber of Commerce and state Chambers of Commerce will help. Most states have economic or industrial expansion departments which also work with local groups. Seek these out for technical know-how and then get going.

WORKING WITH INDUSTRY

Frequently an industry announces it will close shop. Retailers are shocked—among the last to know. Avoid this by working closely with industrialists; stage joint meetings geared toward having them discuss their problems and what retailers can do to help.

Business Calling Cards

This old method still serves a purpose. Benefits include:

LATER REFERENCE

When a customer cannot make up his mind and begins to leave, a salesman offers his card. Within minutes he can mark on it the item, price, measurements, pattern, color, and other vital information. The customer can refer to it later when ordering or comparing.

RENEWED INTEREST

The customer may find the card days later, and it may renew his interest or remind him of a forgotten desire.

EASY TELEPHONE REFERENCE

The card will be a reference if the customer telephones concerning the item. The salesman can be quickly identified.

REORDERING MADE EASY

If the customer wants the item and it has been sold, the notations will make reordering easy.

ESPECIALLY GOOD DURING PROMOTIONS

These are especially helpful during promotions when the hustle and bustle of the event makes it difficult for salesmen to remember customers and their preferences.

Electronic Media

Many retailers don't take advantage of the electronic media and what they can do. Included are:

TELEPHONE BUYING

Telephone company officials will explain how television-telephone combinations can be used for selling—and for buying. Some manufacturing firms now offer this buying service meaning retailers can order from the picture on the tube.

Keep abreast of these innovations by having area representatives of the telephone company in annually to explain their new equipment.

TV WORKSHOPS

Use TV as the media to hold workshops or schools. Short courses can be offered for various members of the family with programs originating at the store.

LIGHTING

Use new and novel approaches. Local electricians or representatives of power companies will be glad to spend the time to make recommendations and share ideas. Add some high voltage to the next promotion with a light show or psychedelic lighting.

CLOSED-CIRCUIT TV

Shoppers see themselves on TV while they shop. It's great fun.

SPECIAL TELEPHONE REPORTS

Use records and special telephone numbers to provide customers with up-to-the-last-minute information about things in which they are interested. In a fishing area, use fishing information; perhaps ski conditions in a winter resort area.

TELEPHONE SALES

These are also good, and clerks with spare time can be put to work telephoning customers with special bargains.

Put the Store on Wheels

Bring back the peddler approach—if not for selling, for service.

VANS MAKE GOOD MINI-STORES

Vans and buses make good mini-stores which can be run into outlying areas. An attraction in themselves, they will spur impulse buying.

Use a horn or bell. Advertise the service and let customers call in to tell what items they want to see when the van comes their way. Use specific runs on specific days so customers can watch for the mini-store. Use an "in the front door out the rear door" policy so customers enter and keep moving, with one or two stops per block.

SERVICE ON WHEELS

Instead of having the customer take the item to the store, bring the service department to the customer by housing it in a van or bus.

Windows

Windows are good promotional and advertising media. In addition to ideas incorporated into gimmicks earlier in this book, window gimmicks include:

LIVE MODELS

These add action. Use them now and then to liven windows up.

DISPLAY-MATERIAL INDEX

Keep a file of items available from various sources, even residents, in the community, which might be loaned for window display use. This will insure that windows are unique and interesting.

Fashion Shows

These lend themselves well to promotions but, they can become old hat; many retailers feel they are being overdone, especially because area clubs and groups hold them as fund-raising events with no innovations.

Stores using these can improve them by adding novel touches, including:

ADD NEW LIFE

Spark new enthusiasm. Try a pajama-party fashion show.

Or use a fashion show to introduce unrelated items, like bedspreads which are worn draped over the models.

Add fishing and hunting gear to sports shows. Add novelty and humorous touches to the show; get away from the rigid formality and let models clown around; add humor with skits and light entertainment.

HOLD IN UNUSUAL PLACES

Break the monotony and hold in unusual places. A bank lobby could be used for a bridal show with the theme "How To Get The Most Wedding For Your Money," etc.

Miscellaneous Ideas

PATRIOTIC TOUR

Sponsor a patriotic tour, busing customers on a tour of area historic sites with buses leaving the store every hour or two.

VACCINATIONS

Keep customers healthy. If the community has no public-health immunization program, retailers can provide one. Area doctors and nurses may donate time and set the program up, with retailers paying for the vaccine.

SALUTE A GOOD NEIGHBOR

Salute the unsung heroes of the community now and then by doing a profile display on them. Find persons who do something for others without expecting anything in return, like the man who used his snowmobile to deliver medicine during a blizzard, the family with children of their own who took in a neighbor's during a tragedy. Ferret these out and honor them.

MYSTERY ENVELOPE FOR PREFERRED CUSTOMERS

Send regular customers a letter with a sealed mystery envelope, explaining the sealed envelope has a discount offer inside. It cannot be opened until purchases are made on a specific day usually. Then the clerk opens the envelope and applies the mystery discount, which can range from ten to 25 percent.

Have "shopping spree" cards in some envelopes, instead of discount offers. These entitle the customer to $25 or $50 in merchandise, with no purchase required at any time in the future.

WRITE YOUR OWN DEAL

Let customers write their own deals on any item in the store. These can be dickered over immediately, or they can be put into a box and checked later with the store calling those in which they are interested.

SHORT-TIME SALES

Use short time blitzes to move merchandise quickly. A three-hour sale in the evening is good. Or hold these for short time periods during busy hours, like 20 minutes on a Sunday afternoon. Announce over the PA system that for the next 20 minutes a specific item will be drastically reduced.

PRIVATE LABEL

Another oldie that is still good. This can add a touch of exclusiveness, and it also makes for good advertising.

PHOTOGRAPH SHOPPERS

Shoot candids of shoppers for later display in store windows. You might work in a contest wherein those who come in and find their picture on display inside the store receive a gift.

EMPLOYING THE HANDICAPPED

Make room for the handicapped, trying to find jobs suitable to them. If every retailer employs a few, it will be a big aid to the community.

REMODELING

Reverse the "closed during remodeling" policy and let curious customers see what is going on. This will build enthusiasm for the time the store reopens.

Index

261